ISBN: 9781314386295

Published by:
HardPress Publishing
8345 NW 66TH ST #2561
MIAMI FL 33166-2626

Email: info@hardpress.net
Web: http://www.hardpress.net

ÎSHA UPANISHAT

TANTRIK TEXTS

Under general Editorship of ARTHUR AVALON.

Vol. I. TANTRÂBHIDHÂNA with BÎJANIGHANTU- and MUDRÂNIGHANTU.

Vol. II. SHATCHAKRANIRÛPANA of Pûrnânanda Svâmî, with Commentary of Kâlîcharana and notes by Shangkara. PÂDUKÂPANCHAKA, with Commentary of Kâlîcharana. With these are notes from the Tikâ of Vishvanâtha on the Second Patala of Kaivalya Kâlikâ Tantra.

Vol. III. PRAPANCHASÂRA TANTRA.

Vol. IV. KULACHÛDÂMANI NIGAMA.

Vol. V. KULÂRNAVA TANTRA.

Vol. VI. KÂLÎVILÂSA TANTRA.

Vols. VII. VIII. TANTRARÂJA. (*In the Press*).

Vol. IX. SHRÎ CHAKRA SAMBHÂRA. (*In the Press*).

WORKS ON TANTRA BY ARTHUR AVALON

TANTRA OF THE GREAT LIBERATION (MAHÂ-NIRVÂNA TANTRA). A Translation from the Sanskrit, with Introduction and Commentary.

PRINCIPLES OF TANTRA (TANTRA-TATTVA) Vols. I and II.

GREATNESS OF SHIVA (MAHIMNA STAVA).

WAVE OF BLISS (ÂNANDA-LAHARÎ).

ORIGIN OF THE VAJRAYÂNA DEVATÂS.

STUDIES IN THE MANTRASHÂSTRA.

THE SIX CENTRES AND THE SERPENT FORCE SHATCHAKRANIRÛPANA. (*In the Press*).

OCEAN OF KULA TANTRA (KULÂRNAVA TANTRA). (*In preparation*).

HYMNS TO THE GODDESS (from the Tantra and other Shâstra and Stotra of Shangkarâchâryya) by ARTHUR and ELLEN AVALON.

To be had of—The PUBLISHERS and MESSRS THACKER SPINK & CO., CALCUTTA, MESSRS. GANESH & CO., MADRAS, MESSRS. TARAPOREWALLA, BOMBAY.

ÎSHA UPANISHAT

with a new commentary

BY

THE KAULÂCHÂRYYA SADÂNANDA.

Translated with Introduction

BY

JNANENDRALAL MAJUMDAR

together with a foreword

BY

ARTHUR AVALON.

LUZAC & CO.
46, GREAT RUSSELL STREET, W. C.
LONDON.
1918

PRINTED BY S. C. CHOWDHURY,
MAHAMAYA YANTRA,
CALCUTTA.

FOREWORD.

Some few years ago Mr. Jnânendralal Majumdar brought me a Sanskrit MS. containing an unpublished Commentary of of the Îsha Upanishat. I have here published it for the first time. The author was, I am informed, a Bengali Tântrika Kaulâchâryya of the name of Satyânanda. I was told at the time that other Commentaries might be available. This one appeared to me to be of peculiar value as having been written with all lucidity and boldness from the standpoint of the Advaitavâda of the Shâkta Âgama.

It explains that Brahman or Chit is Nirguna and Saguna. In the former which is pure and perfect Consciousness, there is neither Svagata, Svajâtiya or Vijâtiya Bheda (Mantra 4.) But when associated with Guna, that is from Its energising aspect It manifests as Mind and Matter. The first is the Kûtastha or Svarûpa and the second the Tatastha aspect. There is an apparent contradiction between these aspects; the first being changeless, formless and the other with change and form. There is only one Brahman and, therefore, being changeless It cannot in Itself change into what is different. The Brahman, however, is associated with Its own Mâyâ Shakti of the three Gunas, which Power, being infinite and inscrutable, · evolves into the world. What then is Mâyâ? I have dealt with this subject in my volume " Shakti and Shâkta " in which I have explained the meaning of the concept according to the Mâyâvâda of Shangkara and the Shaktivâda of the Âgama. To this I refer the interested reader. Satyânanda quite shortly and broadly explains Mâyâshakti to be not some unconscious non-real non-unreal mystery, sheltering with, but not Brahman ; but to be a Shakti, one with the possessor of Shakti, (Shaktimân) and therefore Consciousness. He says (Mantra 1) " This Mâyâshakti is Consciousness because Shakti and possessor of Shakti not being different She is not different from Brahman. She again is Mûlaprakriti, the material cause of the world composed of the Sattva, Rajas and Tamas Gunas." In the Commentary to Mantra 7 he says, "Mâyâ who is Brahman (Brahmamayî) and is (therefore) Consciousness (Chidrûpinî) holds in Herself unbeginning Karmik impressions (Sangskâra) in the form of Sattva, Rajas and Tamas Gunas. Hence She is Gunamayî despite Her being Chinmayî. The Gunas are nothing but Chitshakti because there is no second principle. Brahman which is perfect Consciousness creates the world as Mâyâ

composed of these Gunas and then Itself assumes the character
of Jiva therein for the accomplishment of Its world-play." All
is thus at base Consciousness (Chit). There is no unconscious
non-brahman Mâyâ. There is (Mantra 1) nothing Unconscious
in this world for Shruti says "All this is Brahman" and Brah-.
man is Consciousness. But how then is there an appearance
of Unconsciousness? This he says (*ibid*) is due to the fact that
Mâyâ-shakti is a controlled consciousness. It is controlled in
order that Jîvas may enjoy the fruits of their Karma. The
effect of such control—negation. Nishedha, as others call it—
is that Consciousness appears to be limited. As the Commentary to the 8th Mantra says, Âtmâ as Nirguna Kûtastha is
bodiless. But Saguna Âtmâ or Jîva has body. Consciousness
has thus a perfect and imperfect aspect. It is perfect as the
Kûtastha and imperfect as Jîva with mind and body. Yet
Mâyâ-shakti is Herself conscious, for She is one with Shaktimân. She appears in the form of the world as apparently
unconscious matter through Her unscrutable powers by which
She appears to limit Herself as Consciousness (Chidrûpinî).
The One Perfect Consciousness then appears in dual aspect
as mind and body. Both are at base Consciousness and
therefore the objects of worldly experiences are nothing but
Consciousness as object, just as the mind which perceives them
is Consciousness as subject. The one blissful Chit without
distinction is thus through Its power the subject-object. The
stream of worldly experience is nothing but the changeless
Consciousness in either of these dual aspects. Creation
(Mantra 8, 9) springs from desire, that is the Karmik Sangskâra
which in life is the sub-conscious seed of its experience held
during dissolution as the potentiality of all future creative
imagination (Srishtikalpanâ). That power when manifested is
the cause of the three bodies Causal, Subtle and Gross. The
Bhagavatî Shakti "forsakes in part the state of homogeneous
Consciousness and becomes heterogeneous as the three Gunas
and the bodies of which they are composed". The Gunas do
not exist as something separate from Consciousness because
Consciousness is all pervading (*ibid*). Further in creation they
appear from out Brahman and at dissolution merge in It.

In short the objective world has reality but its reality is
that of Consciousness (Chit) of which it is one aspect as the
subject which perceives it is another. Though men do not
realise it, the Self sees the self in every object. This is realised
by Sâdhanâ. In realisation it is not necessary to flee the world
which is indeed the manifested aspect of the one Brahman.
The Commentary says (Mantra 2) that the whole world being

[iii]

Brahman it should be *enjoyed* by *renunciation*, that is, in a manner to bring about renunciation, that is, by not seeking the fruits of action and by abandonment of the false notion that it is different from Âtmâ. The first step therefore towards Siddhi is to have the Consciousness (Vîrabhâva) in all worldly enjoyment that the Sâdhaka is one with Shiva (Shivoham) and Shivâ (Sâham). In this way the sense of a limited self is lost and the knowledge that all is consciousness is gained. And then, as the Commentator (*ibid*) profoundly says, when objects of desire appear as consciousness their character as objects of desire vanishes. Desire exists only for objects, that is for something seemingly different from the Self which seeks them. But when they are known to be the Self there is no object nor desire nor search therefor. In these few words a fundamental principle of the Tântrika Sâdhanâ is enunciated, as in the foregoing summary the chief doctrines of the Âgama are stated. For these reasons, apart from its other merits, this new Commentary on a great Upanishat has value.

Calcutta,

Arthur Avalon.

The 24th May 1918.

INTRODUCTION.

The final authority on which Tantra as every Shâstra rests is Shruti. The world is eternal though it is sometimes manifest and sometimes unmanifest. In dissolution it exists undistinguishable from consciousness, as the potentiality of the creation yet to be. Veda too is eternal, being the seed of the world as idea existing in Îshvara consciousness which emanates in creation as the world-idea or word (shabda), of which the world is the meaning (artha). The first revelation of Veda is thus the cosmic ideation (Srishtikalpanâ) of Îshvara for whom there is no difference of shabda and artha such as exists in the divided consciousness of the Jîva. When, however, the Jîva's mind is purified he sees that the world is nothing but a kalpanâ of Îshvara. This is the secondary revelation of Veda in the minds of the Rishis or seers (drashtâ) who see the truth in the clear mirror of their purified minds and proclaim it in language which as heard by ordinary men is Shruti. The Samhitâs and Brâhmanas are the Vaidik Karmakânda designed to purify the mind and, as Karma, are necessarily dualistic. The Âranyakas including the Upanishads are the monistic Jnânakânda as understood by the minds purified. Every system of Hindu spiritual culture must therefore be in consonance with the teaching of the Upanishads. So the exponents of different systems explain them in the form of commentaries. The one here published is a labour of this kind by a Tântrik Âchâryya. Using Veda in its secondary sense there are other revelations than those contained in the Shâstras which are ordinarily called the Vedas. Even these are not a single revelation, for otherwise the Vedas could have had but one Rishi. They are a collection of fractional revelations in the minds of many Rishis at different times and occasions and expressed in different styles of language. Their compiler was Vyâsa. As Veda in its secondary sense is but the appearance of pure truth in a pure mind occasioned by the necessity of the time there can be no ground for supposing that the Shâstras called the Vedas are the only revelations. As the ages pass and changes take place in the conditions of the world's races revelations are made in the minds of their great men to guide and teach them. These revelations have given rise to the differing religions of the various peoples. The world is yet far from a state in which all its inhabitants are at the same stage of civilization. No present success will therefore follow any attempt to bring the whole world within the fold of a single religion. For this reason Hinduism does not seek to proselytise. Comparative Theology has shown that there are some underlying elements common to all religions. But these by themselves cannot form a system of practical religion capable of guiding and sustaining men of differing capacities and temperaments. Amongst such other revelations and speaking of the Indian Shâstras there are the Dharma Shâstras spoken by Rishis, the Tantra Shâstra and Purânas. This is not to say that all which is contained in any Shâstra so called have the character and authority of revelation. The fundamental truths in all Shâstras are and must be the same but the presentment and application of these truths vary according to the changes in and needs of the Ages. Thus neither the capacity nor the temperament of the people of our time nor its condition permits of the elaborate ritual prescribed by the Vaidik Karmakânda. The spiritual necessities of men also have to some extent changed. This is explained in many places, amongst others, the Mahânirvâna Tantra (I, 20-50 edited by Arthur Avalon). What is there said may have a rhetorical and therefore exaggerated form, a common trait in Indian Literature seeking to enforce truth by emphasis. We may not believe that at one time man was wholly free from wickedness and has gradually degenerated so as to be almost entirely bad at the present time. Life has doubtless always been attended by inherent evils. The Vedas themselves, the scripture of the Satya age, contain accounts of want and poverty, crime, wickedness, wars, disease and death. Yet it is not to be denied that the age which produced the ritualism of the Brâhmanas and the sublime teaching of the Upanishads was an age superior to the present in which so-called civilized man has scarcely time to say his daily prayers and the soul seems to be irretrievably world-bound. This degeneration from the conditions of the glorious Vaidik ages is the fruit of racial Karma. The Brahmavidyâ of the Upanishads has, however, permeated every section of Hindu society in varying degrees and given it a culture which even in the present day of its degeneration sustains the individuality of the race. There has been, notwithstanding all changes, a continuity from the more ancient times until to-day in the basal ideas of the Hindus which are to be found in all Shâstras. Changes have occurred more in the form of expressions and the disciplines by which those ideas were realised. Throughout the Jnânakânda has remained the same. The main principles of it are :—(1) Correlation as cause and effect between the Jîva's Karma and his existence as an individual bound to the world, (2) the chain of Karma which binds the individual is unbeginning but can be brought to an end, (3) transmigration of the individual from body to body until his Karma is destroyed, (4) the individual's connection with the world in which he appears as the enjoyer and the world as the object of enjoyment is thus incidental and not essential, (5) the individual's attachment to the world and his habit of identifying himself with his body are bred of his ignorance of his real free nature, (6) Karma and ignorance work in a circle, Karma breeding ignorance and ignorance breeding Karma, (7) realisation of his true nature and the consequent destruction of ignorance is the caus·· of the destruction of the individual's Karma and his liberation from the bondage and suffering of the world and (8) liberation is the realisation of the truth (however interpreted) that all is Brahma.

These essential principles form the basis of all Shâstras—Dharmashâstra, Purâna, Tantra or Âgama—and form the basis of their Upâsanâkânda which though differing in many respects from the Vaidik Karmakânda are equally effective to develop spirituality in the differing types to which they are applied. This is not to say that there are no points of difference in these Shâstras. Different conceptions are exemplified in the various systems of worship expounded in them. Thus there are some Purânas, such as the Vaishnava Purânas, which are, according to some sects, dualistic and others, such as the Shâkta Purânas, which are unquestionably monistic. So in the Tantras or the Âgama the Shâkta Tantras are pre-eminently Advaita, others are Vishishtâdvaita and so forth. Though the Shâkta Âgama is a Sâdhana Shâstra, it and the Shâkta Purânas teach that while good Karma enables the aspirant to purify himself, Jnâna alone will give liberation which is monistic experience.

Man, however, is naturally a dualist and his Karmayoga presupposes the existence of both Îshvara and Jîva. But what is it which makes the latter different from the former? Pure consciousness or Âtmâ is the same in both. Diversity is then possible only in the unconscious elements which constitute mind and body composed of the gunas of Prakriti. All things exist to serve the purpose of some other ; and Prakriti and its Vikritis exist for the service of the conscious Purusha. Dualistic philosophy holds that Prakriti is a permanent, independent, unconscious Principle, distinct from the conscious Principle, Purusha, of which there are many. This is not the place to enter into the defects of this system which are obvious, it being enough to point out that if Prakriti be a permanent independent Principle then its bondage is real and its influence on Purusha is necessarily permanent and liberation is impossible. Again, that bondage which is real has no beginning but an end and liberation has a beginning but no end. Both these suppositions are, however, opposed to the fundamental principle that what truly exists cannot cease to exist and what does not exist cannot come to exist. Something cannot be nothing and out of nothing cannot come something. What is real cannot be unreal nor can what is unreal be real.

Shruti, moreover, says, "All this is Brahma." How then can we deal with Purusha and Prakriti in order to reach this monistic conclusion ? This duality can be overcome by one or other of the following two ways, namely, *(1) eliminating Prakriti as being nothing or (2) identifying Her with Purusha or consciousness.*

The first method is that of Shangkaráchárya who posits only one reality, Âtmâ or Purusha. He identifies Prakriti with ignorace (ajnâna), holding that the material world has no other existence save in this ignorance. The three gunas are thus constituents of ignorance. Potentially the latter is adrishta and actually it is the material world of desire, objects of desire and means for their attainment, that is, the senses and mind. The essence of creation is thus nothing but ignorance. The latter may be destroyed by knowledge. But what is a reality cannot be destroyed and made unreal. Conversly, what can be destroyed is not a reality. Hence Prakriti or ignorance is not essentially a reality. Yet it appears to be real. This appearance of unreality as reality is the great world-riddle. So Prakriti is called Mâyâ or that by which the impossible becomes possible (Aghatanaghatanapatîyasî). It is from the world-standpoint something inexplicable and undefinable (anirvâchya), neither unreal or real ; not unreal because the Jîva feels it to be real and not real because it is transient and unknown in liberation. Mâyâ is real to the ignorant who do not seek to analyze it : it is inexplicable to those who seek to analyze its phantom being. It is a negligible thing (tuchchha) to those who feel that, however much it may appear real to the senses, it is in reality unreal. Shangkara thus treats the world both from the transcendental or spiritual (Pâramârthika) and practical (Vyâvahârika) points of view. The former point of view does not in fact treat of the world at all, for the world from such standpoint being nothing no question arises of its origin and so forth. The origin cannot be given of that which does not exist. The world is a mere seeming. It is only from the lower or practical standpoint that there is the necessity of assuming the existence of the world, discussing its nature and origin and so forth.

The practical point of view is that of ignorance, From this standpoint the world is a great reality affording pleasure and pain to multitudinous Jîvas or imperfect forms of consciousness —Chidâbhâsa as it is called in Mâyâvâda, that is, an image of consciousness distorted by its reflection on ignorance with which it is connected. This ignorance is either the ignorance of the individual unit in creation called Avidyâ or, collectively, is the sum total of the ignorance of the units when it is called Mâya. Chidâbhâsa on Avidyâ is Jîva and on Mâyâ Îshvara. Great is the difference between them since in Avidyâ the gunas have lost their equilibrium whereas in Mâyâ they are in equilibrium. Jîva, as the Kulârnava Tantra says, is bound by the bonds (that is, gunas of Avidyâ), Maheshvara is free of them. Ignorance is the cause of the world. But it is not the ignorance of anyone Jîva, for in that case the liberation of a Jîva would mean the disappearance of the world or there would be different worlds for different Jîvas. It is, therefore, the collective ignorance which is the material cause of the world. But ignorance, whether individual or collective, must have consciousness to rest upon. This consciousness is in the case of individual ignorance called Jîva and in the case of collective ignorance Îshvara. In collec-- tive ignorance there can be no inequilibrium of gunas, for in that case it would provide worldly happiness and pain and become individual and cease to be collective, and this larger individual ignorance with the smaller ones would form another collective ignorance and so on indefinitely. Nor can it be said that the happiness and pain provided by the collective ignorance is nothing but the sum total of the happiness and pain provided by the individual items of ignorance, for the ignorance of different Jîvas gives rise to diverse forms of happiness and pain out of the same act so that if they could be totalled at all the total would be zero. The Chidâbhâsa which constitutes Îshvaratva is almost an exact likeness of true consciousness on account of its being associated with Prakriti in equilibrium and consequently unperturbed by the gunas in action. He is Saguna Brahma whilst true consciousness is Nirguna Brahma.

Now, this Chidâbhâsa, which is thus the creator and enjoyer in the world as Îshvara and Jîva, must be, even in its falseness, an emanation from true consciousness, and of this emanation true consciousness must, on account of its perfect conscious nature, be conscious. Again, true conciousness or Nirguna Brahma being the only one existence, the three gunas consti- tuting ignorance must, even though they are unreal, have Nirguna Brahma as the source of their unreal existence, and Nirguna Brahma being all conciousness must be conscious of this fact of unrealities drawing their existence from it. Again, it must be Nirguna Brahma, which causes Chidâbhâsa, an unreality, to appear as real consciousness and operate in the Vyâvahârika world as the doer, enjoyer, sufferer and so forth. All this seems an oxymoron on account of the contradictory character of Nirguna Brahma or Âtmik consciousness and the ignorance or unconsciousness which constitutes the three gunas or Prakriti. But to explain the Vyâvahârika existence of the world, we must take it all for granted in spite of seeming contradiction. The power (Shakti) of pure unlimited consciousness is infinite (ananta) and inscrutable (achintya). No worldly or Vyâvahârika law can put a limitation to the free Shakti of Brahma. The unreal world draws its unreal existence from the sole Brahma reality. It is a vision in Brahma (Brahmakalpanâ) having no independent existence and yet different from it. It should, however, be remembered that all this is connected with the practical point of view of the existence of the world. So long as the world is considered existing, it must be existing in Âtmâ (âtmastha), although it is essentially different from Âtmâ (Âtmavilakshana) and does not exist for its purpose. In reality, however, the world is non-existent and pure Âtmik consciousness is not cognisant of it. Hence the whole question of the cause of the world is a question bred of ignorance or Mâyâ, and has absolutely no connection with pure Âtmik consciousness. Ignorance or Mâyâ, so long as it is supposed to be existing, has also to be supposed to be possessed of the power of receiving an influence from Âtmâ which enables it to evolve the world out of itself. In this creation of the world Âtmik consciousness is neither an instrumental nor a material cause, but is merely an efficient cause, exerting an influence on ignorance or Mâyâ by virtue of its proximity (sannidhimâtrena upakâri). But even this idea of Âtmik consciousness being the efficient cause of creation is a false idea, proceeding, as it does, from a search for the cause of creation which is really non-existing. From the spiritual point of view, there is no world and no creation. Âtmâ alone exists. The Vedântist of Shangkara's school speaks of an inscrutable Shakti of Âtmâ being the cause of creation simply to provide the Vyâvahârika world, that is to say, the world of the worldly man, with a worldly interpretation of its worldly existence. It is the effect of looking at Brahma through the world.

The above is a short exposition of what may be called Shangkara's Vedântism, the keynote of which is :—

"Brahma is true, the world is false.
Jiva is Brahma and none else."

It remains to consider the second possible way of reducing dualism to monism, namely,

2. *Identifying Prakriti with Purusha or consciousness.*

The Prakriti of Shangkara's Vedântism is unconscious and cannot consequently be in any way identified with consciousness. To identify Her with consciousness, we must, consequently, look for some other definition for Her.

"After merging Earth in Water, Water in Fire, Fire in Air, Air in Space, and Space in Ahangkâra and Ahangkâra in Mahat Tattva, Mahat should be merged in Prakriti and Prakriti in Âtmâ." (Devî-bhâgavata XI, 8, 9-10.)

Here it is laid down that just as the Vikritis derived from Prakriti can be merged, step by step, in Prakriti, so Prakriti also can be merged in Âtmik consciouscess. This is layayoga, that is, unity caused by merging. But it is impossible for a thing to be merged in and loose itself in that which is wholly contradictory to itself. As darkness is destroyed by light so unconsciousness may be destroyed by consciousness, but just as darkness cannot be said to be merged in light so unconsciousness cannot be said to be merged in consciousness. It cannot also be said that the word "laya" in the above verses means destruction and not merging, for the Vikritis are not destroyed by Prakriti but are merged in Her in an order inverse to that in which they were derived from Her. Hence the Devîbhâgavata defines Prakriti as :—

" 'Pra' denotes excellence and 'kriti' denotes creation. Therefore, that Devî is called Prakriti who excels in creation. By Yoga He who is Âtmâ appeared as two for the purpose of creation. The right half of His body is called Purusha and the left half Prakriti. She (Prakriti) too is Brahma itself and She is also everlasting and eternal. And as Âtmâ is so is Shakti (Prakriti) just as heat is in fire. Hence, great yogis make no distinction between female (Prakriti) and male (Purusha). All is Brahma and, O great Nârada, ever-existing too." (Devî-bhâgavata IX, 1, 5, 9-11.

"Thus Shakti is all-pervading. She should be considered as Brahma. She should be worshiped in various ways, and be always pondered upon by wise men." Devîbhâgavata I, 8, 34.

"Shakti creates the Universe. It is She who maintains all.

And it is She also who, by Her will, destroys this world composed of moving and non-moving things." Devîbhâgavata I, 8, 37.

Prakriti or Shakti thus identified with consciousness is again considered Nirguna as well as Saguna.

"Wise men say that She is both Saguna and Nirguna. As Saguna She is worshiped by men attached to the world. As Nirguna She is worshiped by men who have no attachment." Devîbhâgavata I, 8, 40.

Saguna and Nirguna Shakti are defined as follows :—

"O Shambhu, I am always the cause and never the effect. I am Saguna on account of being the cause and I am Nirguna when I am merged in Purusha." Devîbhâgavata III, 6, 71.

Nirguna Shakti and Nirguna Purusha are both spoken of as perfect conciousness :—

"Nirguna Shakti is hard to reach and so is Nirguna Purusha. But by Munis they can be reached by knowledge and meditated upon also. Always know Prakriti and Purusha to be unbeginning and indestructible. By faith they can be known and never by want of faith. What is consciouness in all beings, know that to be Paramâtmâ (Supreme Âtmâ), the Light (tejas) which, O Nârada, spreads everywhere and stably resides in various forms of existence. Him and Her, O high-souled One, know to be all-extending and all-pervading. Nothing exists in the world, devoid of them. They should always be thought of as existing, mingled in the body, always imperishable, both the same, both conscious Âtmâ, both Nirguna and both pure. Shakti is the same as Paramâtmâ and Paramâtmâ is the same as Shakti. Devîbhâgavata III, 7, 10-15.

In the Gîtâ, Bhagavân says :—

"I (Parabrahma) am the source of all ; all evolves from Me ; thus comprehending, the wise, who are mindful (of the supreme truth), worship Me." Gîtâ X, 8.

"He, the Supreme Purusha, O Pârtha, may be reached by unswerving devotion, in whom all beings exist and by whom all this (world) is pervaded." Gîtâ VIII, 22.

Prakriti is called Purusha's own :—

"All beings, O Kaunteya, enter into My own Prakriti at the end of a Kalpa, and I create them again at the beginning of a Kalpa. Ruling My own Prakriti, I create again and again.' Gîtâ IX, 7-8.

Prakriti is spoken of, in Gîtâ, as of two kinds, Aparâ (inferior) and Parâ (superior), corresponding to Saguna and Nirguna stated above :—

"Earth, water, fire, air, space, mind, intellect and egoism, these are the eight-fold division of My Prakriti. Aparâ (inferior) is this. Know My other Prakriti, the Parâ (superior), who is Jîva (consciousness) and by whom, O mighty-armed this world is upheld. Know these to be the source of all beings. I am the source of all the world as well as the dissolution." Gîta VII, 4-6.

"Know that Prakriti and Purusha are both without beginning, and know also that Vikritis and attributes are all born of Prakriti. Prakriti is called the cause of the generation of cause and effect. Purusha is called the cause of the enjoyment of pleasure and pain." Gîtâ XIII, 19-20.

Thus the word Prakriti is used in two senses. In its wider sense it includes both the source of the Enjoyer Purusha or Jîva and the source of the world composed of the three gunas. In its narrower sense it means only the latter. Purusha (nirguna) is Nirguna Prakriti and Prakriti in its narrower sense is Saguna Prakriti as defined before.

"I give heat ; I hold back and send forth the rain. O Arjuna, I am immortality and death, and Sat (effects) and Asat (cause)." Gîtâ IX, 19.

The above verses express the same doctrine as that taught in the Shâkta Tantras. The doctrine above illustrated according to which Prakriti is identified with Purusha or consciousness is clearly set forth in the following commentary of Satyânanda on Îshopanishad.

Satyânanda first of all clearly points out that there is in reality nothing unconscious in the world. In his commentary on the First Mantra of the Îshopanishad he says :—

2

"Although in a worldly view things of the world are worldly, in a spiritual view they are considered to be consciousness. It is the Mâyâshakti of Brahma, which is possessed of infinite and inscrutable powers, which evolves as the world. And *this Mâyâshakti is consciousness*, because Shakti and possessor of Shakti not being different, She is not different from Brahma. She, again, is Mûlaprakriti, the material cause of the world composed of the Sattva, Rajas and Tamas Gunas. This Shakti *controls her own consciousness and appears as unconsciousness* in order to enable Jîvas to enjoy the fruits of their Karma. In reality, however, *there is nothing unconscious in the world*, as Shruti says, 'Certainly all this is Brahma' and so forth."

This view is fully borne out by the researches of modern science, specially those of Dr. Jagadîsh Chandra Basu on plant *Bose* life. Our commentator to establish his affirmation brings out a mass of evidence from the Shruti and Smriti. All that seems unconscious is, in reality, imperfectly conscious, and this imperfection in consciousness is the one mystery in creation arising from the inscrutable power of Brahma-consciousness which creates the imperfect consciousness out of and yet without any loss to itself. Karma, birth, death and so forth belong to this imperfect consciousness. All the diversity in the world appertains to imperfect consciousness, while perfect consciousness is thoroughly homogeneous. Satyânanda puts it as follows (commentary on Mantra 4):—

"In Nirguna Brahma which is pure and perfect consciousness there can be no diversity either in itself (svagata) or in own class (svajâtîya) or in different class (vijâtîya). But when its connection with Gunas becomes manifest, then there appear in it, as the Supreme Îshvara possessed of infinite and inscrutable powers, diversities in itself (svagata) appertaining to its secondary aspect.' And, again, "Brahma assumes the aspect of Mâyâ and, producing the movement (kshobha) of desire for creation in itself, creates the world, constantly changing, out of that movement."

Thus the term Mâyâ is, in this theory, used for Brahma itself when Brahma appears as the source of creation. As the source of creation Brahma has in itself the seeds of creation, namely, the three gunas, which also are nothing but consciousness. Hence Satyânanda says (commentary on Mantra 4):—

"As Brahma, which is without a second, is only consciousness, it cannot change into what is different. Nevertheless, on

* Jagadas Chundar Bose,
Response in Living and Non-Living

account of its being possessed of inscrutable powers, it appears as Mâyâ in creation. Mâyâ, who is Brahma (Brahmamayî) and *is consciousness* (Chidrûpinî), holds in Herself un-beginning Karmik impressions in the form of Sattva, Rajas and Tamas Gunas. Hence She is Gunamayî despite Her being Chinmayî. *The Gunas also are nothing but Chitshakti on account of the absence of any second principle.* Brahma who is perfect consciousness creates the world in the form of Mâyâ composed of these three gunas and then Itself assumes the character of Jîva therein for the accomplishment of its world-play."

Thus in creation Brahma has two aspects, the aspect of perfect consciousness and the aspect which evolves imperfect consciousness. The first is Svarûpabhâva or primary aspect and the second Tatasthabhâva or secondary aspect. The Svarûpabhâva is pure Nirguna Brahma or Âtmâ and the Tatasthabhâva is Saguna Brahma who, in creation, appears as the Creator (Îshvara) and the created.

The contradictory qualities of Nirguna and Saguna Brahma are explained in the commentary on Mantras 4 and 5. Nirguna is inactive, Saguna is active, and so forth. And in Mantra 5 the relative functions of the two as Kûtastha Âtmâ, and Jîva and body, are explained. "He (Âtmâ) becoming Saguna encompasses, in the forms of Jîva and body, Himself in the form of Kûtastha who is white, bodiless, painless, nerveless, pure and sinless" (Mantra 8). Creation is thus an *emanation from Brahma*, and may be illustrated as a system of concentric spheres, Nirguna Kûtastha Âtmâ being the centre with spheres, representing the Jîva, causal body, subtle body and gross body, surrounding it. The consciousness of the outer spheres is more and more imperfect in proportion as they are removed from the central Perfect Consciousness. The consciousness of the inner sphere extends to all the spheres, while that of an outer sphere extends only to the sphere or spheres outside it or is, in the case of the outermost gross body, confined to itself only. Thus the Kûtastha is cognisant of the whole creation, the Jîva is cognisant of itself and the three bodies, the causal body is cognisant of itself and the two other bodies, the subtle body is cognisant of itself and the gross body, and the gross body is cognisant of itself only. In this way consciousness is more or less suppressed in the evolution of the world. Satyânanda puts it as follows (commentary on Mantra 8) :—

" Nirguna Âtmâ who is pure Chit (consciousness) is encompassed by Saguna Âtmâ by means of three bodies characterised by wakefulness, dream and sleep. In spite o being thus encompassed the Âtmâ is really bodiless ; for, although He presides over bodies it is not possible for Him, on account of His having no connection with gunas, to be endowed with the characteristics of bodies. The Chhândogyopanishad says, ' O Maghavan, this body is mortal, in the grasp of death ; it is the seat of this immortal bodiless Âtmâ. Good and evil influence him who has a body. Good and evil do not forsake a thing which has a body. But good and evil do not touch that which has no body.' The meaning is that Âtmâ as Nirguna Kûtastha is bodiless and as Saguna Jîva is possessed of body. The pure consciousness of Saguna Âtmâ is more or less suppressed by the gunas in Himself and thus he becomes a Jîva and a body. Nirguna Kûtastha Âtmâ is encompassed by these Jîva and body aspects of Saguna Âtmâ."

The question then naturally arises, how does perfect consciousness become imperfect? This question the commentator answers as follows :—

" It is the opinion of all Upanishads that only one principle exists and nothing else. This principle is Brahma which is consciousness. In creation this consciousness appears in every body both in perfection and in imperfection. In perfection it is Kûtastha and in imperfection it is Jîva and body. How does perfect consciousness become imperfect? Beause of its unbeginning Creative Shakti (Srishtishakti), possessed as it is of inscrutable Shaktis. Is this Shakti consciousness or something different from consciousness? She (Srishtishakti) is consciousness on account of there being actually no difference between a Shakti and the possesor of a Shakti. How does creative Shakti who is consciousness take away (lit. reduce) consciousness? We have said, because Brahma is possessed of inscrutable Shaktis."

Shangkara's Vedântism also expains the world by the inscrutable Shakti of Brahma. But it further holds that in reality the world does not exist and consequently no such Shakti of Brahma is actually displayed. In the present view, however, the world is a real outcome of the actual display of such a Shakti of Brahma. It is Brahma's creative play. Says Satyânanda (commentary on Mantra 8) :—

" It is owing to the Karmik impressions of Jivas consisting of desires for enioyment that the phenomenal world (prapancha) appears in vyâvahâra as unconscious. Under the influence of impressions Jîvas desire enjoyment, and the phenomenal world of enjoyment appears for the satisfaction of these desires. It is owing to the imperfect consciousness of Jîvas that they desire enjoyment and regard the phenomenal world as uncon-scious and enjoyable. Hence impressions (sangskâra) are the cause of Jîvas' imperfect consciousness. These impressions are composed of gunas and evolved (parinâma) out of gunas. Mâyâ, the Gunamayî Creative Shakti of Brahma, *covers Her own perfect consciousness* in the aspect of Karma and Karmik impressions and appears as Jîva and so forth. This is Brahma's creative play. 'He desired, I shall become many for creation. He performed tapas. Performing tapas He created all this, everything that is in the world. Creating it He entered into it'— this Shruti proves that the creation is derived from desire, that is, Karmik impression, and tapas, that is, knowledge. Hence there are *two aspects of Mâyâ*, who may also be called Creative Shakti, Mûlaprakriti or Saguna Brahma, namely, the aspect of desire and the aspect of knowledge. In the aspect of desire She is composed of the three gunas *(trigunâtmikâ)* and in the aspect of knowledge She is consciousness *(chinmayî)*. As composed of the three gunas, She is the cause of the gross, subtle and causal bodies and, as consciousness, She is the cause of all sensations and perceptions in the bodies. *The three gunas also are not different from consciousness.* In dissolution they exist in the form of Brahma   *   *   *   *   *   And at the end of dissolution also the gunas exist as consciousness, in a state of equilibrium, as the self of Îshvara (Îshvarâtmanâ), for which reason Îshvara is possessed of the qualities of omniscience, rulership and so forth. Shruti says, 'They (the Yogîs) saw the Shakti who is the Deva (shining Brahma), hidden by Her own gunas,' that is, the primary aspect of Creative Shakti in which She is perfect Brahma-consciousness is hidden when She appears as the three gunas. For the purpose of creation this Bhagavatî Shakti forsakes, in part, the state of equilibrium and homogeneity (ekarasatva), and becomes heterogeneous as three gunas by virtue of Her possessing inscrutable powers. Hence the world, in which She, again, enjoys as Jîva owing to Her connection with the gunas in inequilibrium and rules everything as Îshvara owing to Her connection with the gunas in equili-brium. Never do the gunas exist separated from consciousness, because consciousness is all-pervading. Hence the theory of their being different from consciousness becomes untenable, as also for the reason that at the end of dissolution they appear out of Brahma, which is consciousness, and, again, at dissolution merge into It."

This is the scheme of creation outlined by Satyânanda by identifying Prakriti with consciousness. The outstanding points in this scheme are :—

(1). One only Principle exists and that is Consciousness.

(2). There is nothing unconscious in the world.

(3). What seems unconscious is in reality imperfectly conscious.

(4). Perfect consciousness is thoroughly homogeneous without any svagata, svajâtîya or vijâtîya diversities.

(5). Inperfect consciousness is heterogenous, being possessed of svagata diversities.

(6). Perfect consciousness is Brahma and is possessed of unlimited and inscrutable powers.

(7). By virtue of its being possessed of such powers perfect consciousness is capable of suppressing its consciousness to a certain extent and appearing as imperfectly conscious.

(8). When it assumes the role of suppressing its consciousness to a certain extent, perfect consciousness receives the names of Srishtishakti, Mûlaprakriti, Prakriti or Îshvara.

(9). Srishtishakti, Prakriti or Îshvara is perfect consciousness, but evolves imperfect consciousness out of itself.

(10). The elements of imperfect consciousness are the three gunas, Sattva, Rajas and Tamas.

(11). In Prakriti they exist in a state of equilibrium. In creation they are in inequilibrium.

(12). The effect of the gunas being in inequilibrium are the Jiva and the bodies.

(13). The Jîva is the cogniser under the influence of the three gunas in inequilibrium and the bodies are the means and objects of cognition composed of them.

(14). Prakriti thus considered the cause of the world is Saguna Prakriti as defined above in the quotation from the Devîbhâgavata. In Pralaya or dissolution this Saguna Prakriti becomes Nirguna. She is Gunamayî (Srishtishakti) as well as Chinmayî (Chitshakti). In creation She is manifest as both. In dissolution Her gunamaya aspect is merged in her chinmaya aspect.

The two views described above as those of Shangkarâ-châryya and Satyânanda, in which Prakriti is respectively held as unconsciousnesss and consciousness, are apparently contradictory. But, nevertheless, each has its place in Advaita spiritual cutlture.

Shangkarâchâryya's position is that of a man who has risen above Karma. As the Gîtâ (III-17) says, "But the man who rejoices in Âtmâ and is satisfied with Âtmâ and is content in Âtmâ, for him no duty exists". Âtmâ is perfect consciousness. A man who is established in Âtmâ may, from the monistic stand-point, be said to be not cognisant of imperfect consciousness or unconsciousness. To him the world does not exist, because perfect Âtmik consciousness is not in the world. Very important is the passage in the Devîbhâgavata which says, "O Shambhu, I am always the cause and never the effect" (III-6-7 quoted above). Prakriti who is identified in the Devîbhâgavata with perfect consciousness is the cause and never the effect which is the world. Hence to him who is established in the cause, the effect may be said to be non-existing. The Gîtâ says : —

"Know that the Bhâvas (states) that are Sâttvik, Râjasik and Tâmasik are from me ; not I in them, but they in me.

All this world, deluded by these Bhâvas composed of the three gunas, knows not me who is above these and imperishable.

This divine Mâyâ of mine, composed of the gunas, is hard to cross. They who come to me, they cross this Mâyâ". Gîtâ VII. 12-14.

"By me, in my unmanifested aspect, all this world is pervaded. All beings are seated in me. I am not seated in them.

Nor are beings seated in me. Behold my Yoga of Îshvara-hood ! The support of beings yet not seated in beings, I am myself their Generator". Gîtâ IX, 4-5.

Behind the world of unconsciousness or imperfect consciousness is perfect Âtmik consciousness, but behind perfect Âtmik consciousness there is no world.

The same thing is said in the Chhândogya Upanishad in a very important and well-known passage, namely, "Wherein is He, the Lord, established? In His own greatness or perhaps not in greatness".

It is doubtless easy to say, "The world is Brahma"; but to realise it is beyond ordinary powers. On realisation it ceases to exist as the world which was known to us. If, therefore, one is called to explain the Universe with all its variety, the only answer can be Mâyâ —an unexplainable manifestation of Brahma as non-Brahma yet nothing in truth but Brahma. It is thus anirvâchya, or avitarkya as the Mahânirvâna Tantra calls it. It is also on this anirvâchya doctrine that Satyânanda stands, for the fact that consciousness has clouded itself and materialized can only be accounted for by the existence of Achintya Shakti which both systems must ultimately assume. The difference between the two arises perforce from the fact that, unlike Shangkara, Satyânanda speaks for those who look at the question from the world standpoint. In fact, Satyânanda's theory is that of monistic Karmayoga. To men who have not attained to the sublime height of self realisation the world can not be nothing, however much they may be monists from the merely intellectual point of view. Satyânanda's commentary is written from their standpoint. Having direct realisation of the world only and a mere indirect knowledge of perfect conscious-ness, their monism consists in training their minds to regard the world as a manifestation of Brahma and, *in this sense*, Brahma itself. The underlying principle is stated in the Gîtâ (XIII, 30), "When he perceives the diversified existences of beings as rested in one and proceeding therefrom, then he attains to Brahmahood."

Satyânanda's commentary is of great value as indicating the philosophy underlying Tântrik Sâdhana of the Advaita school and as· showing that that Sâdhana is in principle Vedântik. The aim of such Sâdhana is to achieve monism through dualism, the practice of dualistic Karma under the inspiration of the monistic idea. And so on waking the Shâkta Sâdhaka says:— "I am, O Devî, Brahma and none other." By such monism is held not by the elimination of Prakriti out of existence but by identifying her with Purusha. The Mahânirvâna Tantra (Second Ullâsa) first speaks of the Svarûpa Bhâva of Brahma as pure Chit, and the Devî is described as the Parâ Prakriti of Brahma. Then the world is said to draw its existence from Brahma. The aspect of Brahma in which It appears as Îshvara, Jîva and the world is the secondary aspect or Tatastha Bhâva.

That is set forth clearly by Satyânanda in the commentary on Mantra 8. The Kulârnava Tantra (First Ullâsa) says, "Sachchidânanda is Nirguna, Jîvas are but portions of Him," by which is meant that in and as Jîvas Brahma appears as imperfect consciousness. So in the Gîtâ (X. 42) Bhagavân says, "I am pervading all the universe with a portion of myself."

Shruti also lends authority to this view when it says, " Pâdosya vishva bhûtâni tripâdasyâmritang divî," that is, "A part of Him appears as all the beings. Three parts of Him are immortal in Heaven." (Purusha Sûkta).

Râghava Bhatta in his commentary on Sâradâtilaka (1. 7) quotes from the Prayogasâra Tantra and Vâyavîyasanghitâ to show that Prakriti is an emanation from consciousness.

"She who is ever-existing, all-pervading and the source of the universe, issued from it." Prayogasâra.

"By the desire of Shiva the Supreme Shakti becomes unified with the Principle of Shiva and at the beginning of creation emanates from it like oil from sesamum." Vâyavîyasanghitâ.

Râghava Bhatta quotes the following also from Shaivadarshana to show that Prakriti and Purusha are not different :—

"Shakti does not exist without Shiva and Shiva does not exist without Shakti. Truly speaking, there is no difference between the two just as there is no difference between the moon and the moon-light."

The Sâradâtilaka by Lakshmanâchâryya deals, in its first two chapters, with the Tantrik Philosophy of creation in the most masterly way. In it "Eternal Shiva" is spoken of as possessed of two aspects, Nirguna and Saguna. The Nirguna aspect is the aspect unconnected with Prakriti and the Saguna aspect is the aspect connected with Prakriti.

"Eternal Shiva is to be known as Nirguna and Saguna. Nirguna is unconnected with Prakriti, Saguna is said to be associated with Prakriti." Sâradâtilaka I. 6.

In the next verse it is said that the world evolves out of Saguna Shiva who is as much Sachchidânanda as Nirguna Shiva.

"Out of the Supreme Îshvara associated with Prakriti and possessed of the wealth of Sachchidânanda, there appeared Shakti, out of Shakti appeared Nâda and out of Nâda Bindu."

The appearance of Shakti or Prakriti out of Îshvara associated with Prakriti is explained by the commentator Râghava Bhatta to mean that "the eternal Prakriti who was lying in a subtle state in the greater dissolution identified with consciousness became ready for creating the world of Sâttvik, Râjasik and Tâmasik persons and things by causing a disturbance in the equilibrium of the gunas."

Thus the eternality of Prakriti is recognised. Lower down in verses 11 and 12 it is said that out of the Supreme Bindu (derived from Shakti as stated above) appeared Shabdabrahma.

"Out of the dividing Supreme Bindu arose the unmanifested sound which wisemen versed in all Âgamas call Shabdabrama."

And then in verse 13 this Shabdabrahma is considered the consciousness in all beings.

"It is my opinion that Shabdabrahma is the chaitanya (consciousness) of all beings."

Thus the consciousness in all beings, the jîva-consciousness, is derived from Prakriti.

Lower down, again, in verse 17 and the following verse the creation of the tattvas—mahat, ahangkâra, mind, the indriyas, the subtle bhûtas and the gross bhûtas—which form the ingredient of the material to which the jîva-consciousness spreads is deprived from the same Supreme Bindu.

"Then from the fundamental unmanifested Supreme Being, when changed, there appeared the tattva called Mahat consisting of the gunas and the source of mind and so forth."

Thus Prakriti is, according to the Sâradâtilaka, the source of both the jîva-consciousness and the objects of jîva-consciousness composed of the three gunas in inequilibrium.

This is exactly what Satyânanda says in his commentary on Mantra 8:—"Hence there are two aspects of Mâyâ, who may also be called Creative Shakti, Mûlaprakriti or Saguna Brahma, namely, the aspect of desire and the aspect of knowledge. In the aspect of desire She is composed of the three gunas and in the aspect of knowledge She is consciousness. As composed of the three gunas She is the cause of the gross, subtle and causal bodies and as consciousness She is the cause of all sensations and perceptions in the bodies."

The monistic dualism of the Tântrik cult is little understood. There seems to be a conflict between Shangkara's Mâyâvâda and Tântrik sâdhana though both are avowedly monistic. Shangkara's Mâyâvâda and Tântrik sâdhana, however, belong to different fields of spiritual realisation and do not consequently cross each other. In the field of sâdhana, Mâyâvâda is more a speculation ✓ than a realisation and should not interfere with the sâdhaka's struggle for spiritual achievement by means of Karmayoga. His monistic Jnâna must not be allowed to hamper his Karma. They should go together and thus give the sâdhaka the highest reward of liberation from worldly existence. If the two do not go together, it is better that he should abandon Jnâna, which is ⌞ bound to be in his case but a mere shadow of True Jnâna, and perform Karma than that he should abandon Karma, which alone can raise him by purifying his mind, and hold to that shadow. The Tântrik sâdhana is the sâdhana in which the ✓ two, Jnâna and Karma, join hands to shower spiritual benefit on the sâdhaka.

It may be asked, where is the authority for this coalition between these natural enemies, Jnâna and Karma ? The Tantra Shâstra, which is believed by its followers to be true Revelation, no doubt furnishes this authority. But the authority of the Tantra itself will be of no account and fall through if it contradicts the first and foremost revelation, the Shruti. The value of the present commentary consists in this that it shows that the Tântrik principle of monistic dualism which allows of a coalition between Jnâna and Karma is advocated for sâdhakas in the Shruti. The Îshopanishad distinctly says :—

"Vidyâ and Avidyâ, he who knows the two together surpasses death by Avidyâ and tastes of immortality by Vidyâ." Avidyâ means Karma and Vidyâ means Jnâna. Being accompanied by Karma this Jnâna is the Devatâjnâna of the sâdhaka, that is to say, his Jnâna that the Devatâ he worships in his Karma is Supreme Brahma. He can perceive Brahma only through the Devatâ he worships. Brahma is not an object of his direct perception. But gradually as he practises Karma and Jnâna together, the Karma purifies his mind and enables the light of monistic knowledge to shine on it more and more till ultimately through perfect purification of the mind the sâdhaka, becoming free from attachment to worldly enjoyment, is free from descent to the mortal world and through the perfection of monistic knowledge directly realises the one Brahma, Which is the true immortality.

There is thus a sequence in the effects of Karma and Jnâna in the upward elevation of the spirit till liberation is attained. Karma purifies the mind and places the sâdhaka on the path to liberation from which there is no fall to this mortal world, while Jnâna alone gives absolute liberation in which the individual attains Nirvâna, that is, merging in and unification with the one homogeneous Brahma existence. This Jnâna is Aparoksha Jnâna, that is, direct realisation of Brahma, and should not be confounded with the Devatâjnâna, explained above, which is Paroksha Jnâna, or indirect knowledge of Brahmahood, coalescing with Karma to purify the sâdhaka's mind and establish him in Aparoksha Jnâna. There can be no association of Karma with Aparoksha Jnâna, for its attainment is tantamount to the liberation of the Jîva. This matter is very clearly dealt with by Satyânanda in his commentary on Mantra 9. There is, in fact, an antagonism between Karma and Aparoksha Jnâna. Where there is Karma there is no Aparoksha Jnâna and where there is Aparoksha Jnâna there is no Karma. It must, however, be understood that hereby Karma is meant sakâma or nishkâma Karma done by one who has no Aparoksha Jnâna. All such Karma bind the Jîva to individual existence, however highly placed that existence may be. But he who possesses Aparoksha Knowledge is liberated even in life, so that whatever he may do is a mere activity of his senses without binding effect, for the individual having become one with Eternal Brahma there is none whom it can bind, as explained by Satyânanda in his commentary on Mantra 2.

CALCUTTA.

JNANENDRALAL MAJUMDAR.

The 18th January, 1918.

TRANSLATION

OF

ÍSHA=UPANISHAD.

AND

SATYÁNANDA'S COMMENTARY

WITH

OCCASIONAL NOTES,

ÎSHA UPANISHAT

OF THE

WHITE YAJURVEDA known as VÂJASANEYA SANGHITÂ,

TOGETHER WITH THE

COMMENTARY OF SATYÂNANDA.

Satyânanda's introduction to his Commentary.

I bow to Brahma Who has no second, is knowledge itself, is the doer, the enjoyer, the lord, the subtle, the most gross, the cause of the cause of the world (1).

In the Upanishat consisting of eighteen Mantras beginning with " Îshâ vâsyam " the desire-free seeker of liberation is the adhikârî (2), liberation is the necessity, Âtmâ is the subject and indication of the means of liberation by the establishment of the characteristics of Âtmâ is the connection (3). Liberation is the realisation of the true nature (4) of Âtmâ. This realisation is dependant on mental purification. Mental purification also is dependant on Karma. Those who have attained to a realisation of the true nature of Âtmâ are liberated even here. They have no necessity for Karma, nor do they despise Karma. Those, however, who do not know Âtmâ on account of their minds being impure should perform Karma selflessly and with resignation to Îshvara

---

(1) The cause of the world is Prakriti, and Brahma is the cause of Prakriti.

(2) Person competent to study this Upanishat.

(3) Every book to be useful must fulfil four primary conditions. (*a*) It must deal with a specific subject. (*b*) It must he intended to fulfil a necessity. (*c*) There must be persons competent to study it. And (*d*) there must be a true connection between the subject and the fulfilment of the necessity.

(4) Svarûpa.

for attaining purification of mind. Those whose minds are, in consequence of such performance of Karma, purified even in this birth become liberated in life and, on death, are merged in Âtmâ itself. Those, however, among the performers of self-less Karma whose mental impurities are not removed in this birth, are, on death, placed on the Devayâna Path, the path of gradual liberation. There they gradually attain purification of mind, live in the Brahmaloka till the end of the Kalpa and are, at its end, merged in Brahma. All this which is in perfect accord with the findings of all Vedânta, we shall explain as we proceed to comment on the Mantras.

ÎSHA UPANISHAT.

BENEDICTION.

Om that is perfect, this is perfect, from the perfect arises the perfect. Taking the perfect of the perfect, it is the perfect that remains (1).

OM PEACE, PEACE, PEACE.

*   *   *   *   *   *

1. By Îsha is to be covered all this, that which is changeful in the changing world. Hence by renunciation it should be enjoyed. Do not crave for anybody's wealth.

Satyânanda's commentary.

All this visible world, consisting of moving and non-moving things and characterised by waste and accretion, should be *covered by*, that is, looked at as, Brahma Which is consciousness. Îsha is the Ruler, the creator, preserver and destroyer of the world. That is, Îshvara. And Îshvara is consciousness by virtue of His character as the doer. Shruti says, "He is the seer, the toucher, the hearer, the smeller, the taster, the thinker, the determiner, the doer, the Purusha who is the cogniser. He is established in the supreme undecaying Âtmâ." By Îshvara, such as He is, the world should be covered. The meaning is that although in a worldly view things of the world are worldly, in a spiritual view they are considered to be conscious. It is the Mâyâshakti of Brahma which is possessed of infinite and inscrutable powers which evolves as the world. And this Mâyâshakti is consciousness. because Shakti and possessor of Shakti not being different, She is not different from Brahma. She, again, is Mûlaprakriti, the material cause of the world composed of Sattva, Rajas and Tamas gunas. This Shakti controls her own consciousness and appears as unconsciousness in order to enable Jîvas to enjoy the fruits of their Karma. In reality, however, there is nothing unconscious in the world, as Shruti says, "Certainly all this is Brahma"; "All this is Âtmâ"; "Purusha is this universe, karma, tapas, Brahma, supreme immortality"; "This Brahma, Which is immortality, is in front, Brahma is behind, Brahma is on the right hand side and on the left. It extends above and below. In fact, this vast universe is Brahma"; and so forth. Wise men whose minds have been purified through exhaustion of the fruits of Karma cover the whole world with Brahma, that is, look at it as Brahma. *World* means the earth and other lokas (2). *Hence*, that is, the whole world being Brahma, it should be enjoyed *by renunciation*, that

---

(1) *That* means Supreme Brahma which is invisible. *This* means the visible world. *This is perfect* in the sense that it is in reality Supreme Brahma. *Taking the perfect*, that is, the Supreme Brahmahood, *of the perfect*, that is, of the world, *it is the perfect*, that is, the One Brahma, *that remains.* This mantra amplifies the dictum, "Certainly all this is Brahma." Brihadâranyakopanishat V. 1, 1.

(2) There are seven lokas, that, is habitations for Jîvas, namely, Bhu, Bhuba, Svah, Maha, Jana, Tapah and Satya. Bhu is the earth.

2.   It is by doing work in this way that one may desire to live here a hundred years.   To you man there is thus no way other than this by which Karma will not stick.

is, in a manner to bring about renunciation, without craving for fruits, by forsaking the idea of its being different from Âtmâ. *Anybody's wealth*, that is, any object of desire belonging to own self or anybody else.   The sense is that when all objects of desire appear as consciousness their character as objects of desire vanishes.   Bhagavân (1) also has said, " When a man abandoneth, O Pârtha, all the desires of the heart and is satisfied in Âtmâ by Âtmâ, then is he called quietminded."

2.   The man who *does work*, that is, allows his senses to operate, *in this way*, that is, with the knowledge that all is Brahma and without craving for fruits, *that one may desire to live here* on earth *a hundred years*, that is, a long life.   The word *you* is used to indicate that this applies to every man.   *There is thus no way other than this*, that is, no way other than selfless work, *by which Karma will not stick*, that is, you will not get the fruits of Karma.   The state of liberation-in-life of those who know Âtmâ is indicated here.   So long as the body exists even no wiseman can live inactive, for he has his senses and is subject to prârabdha (2) Karma.   Bhagavân also says the same to Arjuna, " Nor can any one, even for an instant, remain really inactive, for helplessly everyone is driven to action by gunas (3) born of Prakriti."

Now, it has been said in the First Mantra that he who knows Âtmâ to be Brahma and is liberated in life sees Brahma everywhere even while doing work through the operation of the functions of the body under the influence of Prakriti or for the teaching of men.   In the Katha Upanishat also it is said, " The seat of the Unborn and Ever-conscious has eleven gates.   By working (for Him) one does not grieve, but being liberated, is saved (from rebirth)" (4).   If such a liberated knower of Âtmâ wants to live even a hundred years Karma does not attach to him.   The expression " desire " is here used simply for laudation, to show that no amount of Karma can bind one who is liberated in life.   The conflict between Jnâna and Karma is to be understood to exist in relation to the Sakâma and Niskâma Karma of the ignorant and not in relation to the mere activities of the senses of wisemen (5).   Like the performance of the duties of a Kshatriya by Bhagavân Vâsudeva (6), the activity of the senses of wisemen is not such work as binds the Jivâ to the world-tree.   Smriti (7) says, " Nor do actions attach to Me nor do I desire for the fruits of action " ; " O Dhananjaya (8), actions do not bind him who is self-possessed" ; " He whose Âtmâ

(1) Shrikrishna in the Bhagavadgîtâ
(2) Karma is of three kinds : — (1) Prârabdha, which has began to work and of which the consequence is the present life. (2) Sanchita, that is, stored, which has not yet begun to bear fruits. (3) Kriyamâna, which is being earned by present action.
(3) The Sattva, Rajas and Tamas gunas.
(4) The Unborn and Ever-conscious is Âtmâ.   The seat is the gross body   The eleven gates are the two eyes, the two ears, the two nostrils, the mouth, the navel, the generative organ, the anus and the Brahmarandhra, that is, the aperture at the crest of the head.
(5) Work done by wisemen who know Âtmâ is mere activity of the senses to which he attaches no ahangkâra.
(6) Vâsudeva is Shrikrishna.   He was a Kshatriya and, although an incarnation of Ishvara, performed all the duties of the caste he had assumed.
(7) The Gîtâ Smriti.   (8) Dhananjaya is a name of Arjuna.

3. Asuryya is the name of the lokas covered with blinding darkness. To them they go after death, the men who kill Âtmâ.

---

has become the Âtmâ of all beings is not affected even by doing work" ; and so forth. Shruti says, "The knot (1) of the heart is cut, all doubts are dispelled and all Karma is destroyed of him who has seen Him who is the cause and the effect (2)" ; " When all the desires which harbour in his heart are removed, the mortal becomes immortal and tastes of Brahma even here" ; " When the seer sees the shining Purusha who is the doer, the lord, the source of Lord Brahmâ, then the wiseman is washed clean of virtue and sin and attains supreme equanimity" ; and so forth.

3. After speaking of the state of liberation in life characterised by a thorough knowledge of Âtmâ, in this Mantra the Upanishat speaks of the state of delusion characterised by a thorough want of knowledge of Âtmâ in which one thinks, " consciousness does not shine, it does not exist."(3) Suras are wisemen. Those who are not suras are asuras, throughly devoid of the knowledge of Âtmâ. In the story beginning with " Wherefor Devas and Asuras struggled," the Chhândogyopanishat, by saying that " the Asuras struck (the prâna) with sin, " indicates that they are darkness itself, destitute of the light of Âtma—blind egotism, sinful. The Kathopanishat says, " How can that (Âtmâ) be known from any body other than who believes in its existence," and, " Of the two (upâdhi-ridden Âtmâ and upâdhi-free Âtmâ) (upâdhi-free Âtmâ) should be realised as existing in Truth. The Truth favours him who realises (Âtmâ) as existing." Hence the Upanishat indirectly points to the infidel who does not perceive the existence of Brahma in either svarûpa or tatastha aspect. In the Gîtâ Shâstra also it is said, " Men, who have the nature of Asuras, know neither devotion (to duty) nor abstinence (from evil). Neither cleanliness nor good habit nor truth exists in them. The world, they say, is without truth, without basis (4), without an Îshvara, brought about by mutual union and caused by lust and nothing else (5). Holding these views, these ruined selves of small understanding and fierce deeds prevail as enemies of the world for its destruction," and so forth. *Lokas* having the character of asuras are *asuryya lokas*. The word *loka* is derived from root *lok*, to obtain, and means what is obtained, that is, fruit of Karma consisting of a particular rebirth. Covered *with blinding darkness*, that is, the darkness of delusion (6), devoid of the light of Âtmâ. *The men who kill Âtmâ* are the men who, through delusion of intellect, think that beyond the body, there is no undecaying and undying Âtmâ consisting of consciousness. Fruits of Karma are of three kinds. The Karma which consists in the worship of the tatastha saguna (7) aspect of Brahma-consciousness and is performed with faith and resignation to Îshvara, with a mind

---

(1) The knot of the heart consists of desires.
(2) The cause and the effect is Brahma. The cause is the cause of the world and the effect is the world.
(3) Consciousness does not appear as an independent principle and not an attribute of the physical body. Hence, there is no existence of consciousness as an independent principle.
(4) Basis of dharma and adharma.   (5) This is the view of Chârvâka.
(6) Moha.   (7) The secondary aspect in which Âtmâ has assumed the upâdhi of gunas.

4. Unmoving and one, swifter than the mind, the Devas do not get It as It moves before (them). Running It surpasses others. Non-moving, Mâtarishvâ places all Karma in It.

---

purified by tapas and so forth, leads to Brahmaloka (1) by the Devayâna Path whence there is no return. The men, however, of impure minds who consider heavenly happiness to be the highest object of attainment and to that end perform Yajnas and so forth with a craving for their fruits, their Karma leads them to the Chandraloka by the Pitriyâna Path from which there is a return to this sangsâra. Those, again, who consider the body to be Âtmâ and are devoted to this world and thoroughly deluded, for them there is no journey to the next world either by the Devayâna Path or by the Pitriyâna Path. On the contrary, they take birth and die repeatedly without interruption as insects, flies and other ephemeral creatures. The *lokas* of these ephemeral creatures are asuryya, covered with the blinding darkness of perfect ignorance. Shruti says, "The peaceful men who, living in forests on alms, practice tapas and' shraddhâ and wisemen become taintless and by the solar gate go where resides that immortal Purusha of undecaying self (2)" ; "The deluded men who consider Yajnas and works of public utility as the best and do not know of any thing better, they enjoy on the surface of heaven earned by their good deeds and thereafter enter into this or even a worse loka" ; "Now, to neither of these two paths go these little ephemeral creatures who are born again and again. This is the third place " ; " The means of attaining to the next world is not revealed to the child (3) who is attached to worldly objects and deluded by wealth. This is the world, there is none beyond it—whoever thinks thus comes under my (4) sway again and again " ; and so forth. Smriti also says, " White and black (5), these are thought to be the world's everlasting paths. By the one he goes who returns not, by the other he who returns again" ; " Cast into the wombs of Asuras, deluded birth after birth, attaining not to Me, O Kaunteya, they sink into the lowest depths " ; and so forth.

4. After showing the state of liberation in life of those who possess perfect knowledge and the state of blinding darkness indicated by ephemeral existence of those who are perfectly ignorant, the Upanishat proceeds, in this Mantra, to show the nirguna and saguna conditions

---

(1) The loka of Brahmâ or Hiranyagarbha.
(2) Peaceful men are men whose senses have been withdrawn from their objects—men belonging to the vânaprastha and sannyâsa âshramas.
Tapas—Duties of own âshrama.
Shraddhâ—Knowledge of Hiranyagarbha and others.
Wisemen—Householders who know Panchâgnividyâ, or the science of Five Fires (See Chhândogyopanishat V, 3 ff).
Taintless—free from virtue and sin.
Solar gate—the Devayâna Path.
Immortal Purusha—Hiranyagarbha.
Of undecaying self—living so long as the sangsâra lasts.
(3) Child, that is, one who is senseless like a child.
(4) My, that is, of Death.
(5) The Devayâna Path is called white because knowledge shines in it. The Pitriyâna Path is called dark because there is no light of knowledge in it.

of the primary and secondary aspects (1) of Brahma Which is consciousness. *Unmoving* (anejat), that is, devoid of all change of condition, nirguna. *One* (ekang), that is, without a second, the same at all times and in all things. In Nirguna Brahma Which is pure and perfect consciousness there can be no diversity either in itself or in own class or in different class (2). But when Its connection with gunas becomes manifest, then there appear in It, as the Supreme Îshvara possessed of infinite and inscrutable powers, diversities appertaining to Its secondary aspect. This is said in *swifter than the mind* (manaso javîyah). The *mind* here stands for all the inner senses (3). *Swifter*, that is, extremely restless, changeful. The mind which assumes the shape of a different thing every moment, is the most restless of all worldly things. Brahma assumes the aspect of Mâyâ and producing the movement (4) of desire for creation in Itself, creates the world, constantly changing, out of that movement. "He desired, I shall become many for creation"; "In the beginning there was this Âtmâ alone. Nothing else appeared. He desired, I shall create lokas"; "Out of It appear life, mind and all the senses, space, air, fire, water and earth, the supporter of the universe" —in these and many other places Shruti teaches that Brahma is both the creator and what has to be created. Brahma is swifter than the mind on account of Its being the creator and the created. Whatever form of vritti (5) the mind takes, Brahma first creates Itself as that vritti in order to enable the mind to enjoy the fruits of its Karma according to its impressions (6). *The Dîvas*, that is, the Shining Ones, the deities presiding over the senses, *do not get It*, that is, do not get this Brahma, on account of their Râjasik and Tâmasik impurity. Elsewhere also Shruti says, "He knows the knowable, of Him there is no knower." The Kathopanishat says, "The Self-manifested One (7) smote the senses by making them outward-going. Hence they perceive outward things and not the inner Âtmâ." *As It moves before them*, that is, as It engages Itself in creation prior to the activities of the mind and the senses for their purpose (8). The Kathopanishat also says, "The Purusha who wakes among the sleeping, making objects of desire for them, that is the Light, that is Brahma, that is called Immortality. It is the refuge of all the lokas. None surpasses It." Or (9), because Brahma sends the mind and senses to their respective works, It is said to be moving before them, the activity of the sendor being prior to that of the sent. The Talabkâra Upanishat first asks, "By whom desired and sent does the mind move? By whom engaged does the Prâna first move? By whom desire I do people speak? What Deva does engage the eye and ear?" and then answers, "He who is the ear of the ear, the

(1) Primary—svarûpa. Secondary—tatastha. (2) In itself—svagata. In own class—svajâtiya. In different class—Vijâtiya.
  Svagata diversity is a diversity of the nature of leaves, branches and so forth of a tree. Svajâtiya diversity is a diversity of different individuals of the same class, as of different trees. Vijâtiya diversity is a diversity of different class, as of trees, men, birds, beasts and so forth.
(3) The inner senses are manas, buddhi, chitta and ahangkâra.
(4) Movement—Kshobha.
(5) Vritti—function. Perception of an object means that the mind has functioned as, taken the shape of, that object.
(6) Impression—sangskâra.
(7) Svayambhû, Supreme Ishvara of whom there is no creator.
(8) Objects must be created before the mind and the senses can move towards them.
(9) An alternative meaning. It is the rule with commentators that among many possible meanings, the more appropriate ones are placed later, the most appropriate one coming the last.

5. It moves, It moves not : It is distant, It is near : It is within all this and It is outside all this.

mind of the mind, the speech of the speech, the Prâna of the Prâna, the eye of the eye." This establishes that Brahma is the root of all perceptions. Elsewhere, Shruti says, " He is the seer, the toucher, the hearer, the smeller, the taster, the thinker, the determiner, the doer, the Purusha, who is the cogniser. He is established in the supreme undecaying Âtmâ." In order to bring out the contradictory characteristics of Brahma according as It is saguna or nirguna, again says, *running It surpasses others etc.* *Running* (dhâvatah), that is, becoming active, *It* (tat), that is, Brahma, *surpasses* (atyeti) *others* (anyân), that is, the mind, senses and so forth. After speaking of the saguna aspect, speaks of the nirguna aspect thus. *Non-moving* (tishthat) means that the Brahma Principle is inactive and unchanging. As Brahma, Which is without a second, is only consciousness, It cannot change into what is different. Nevertheless, on account of Its being possessed of inscrutable powers, It appears as Mâyâ in creation. Mâyâ, Who is Brahma (1) and is consciousness (2), holds in Herself unbeginning Karmik impressions in the form of Sattva, Rajas and Tamas gunas. Hence She is Gunamayî despite Her being Chinmayî. The gunas also are nothing but Chitshakti on account of the absence of any second principle. Brahma, which is perfect consciousness, creates the world in the form of Mâyâ composed of these three gunas and then Itself assumes the character of Jîva therein for the accomplishment of Its world-play. As Shruti says, " He created all this, everything that is here. Creating it He entered into it "; " This (world) was non-existence before. Out of it arose existence. Then He created Himself"; and so forth. *Mâtarishvâ*, that is, he who moves in the firmament, that is, Air, that is, Prâna. Prâna *places all Karma*, consisting of Dharma and Adharma, *in It*, Brahma. Prâna, which is activity (3) places all karmas, resting in it, in Brahma, because in reality they are nothing but Brahma.

5. In this Mantra the Upanishat repeats the purport of the last Mantra in order to more clearly put forth the contradictory characteristics of Brahma according as It is Saguna and Nirguna. *It*, Brahma, *moves* (ejati), that is, becomes active owing to connection with the gunas in the aspect of Mâyâ. *It moves not* (naijati), that is, remains inactive owing to want of connection with the gunas in the aspect of perfect consciousness. *It*, Brahma, *is distant*, because in Its nirguna aspect It is unattainable by the mind or the senses. Shruti says, " Which speech fails to reach along with the mind." *It is near*, that is, Brahma is near, because in Its saguna aspect It is everywhere in the world. *It is within all this*, that is, within all visible things of the world in the aspect of conscious Âtmâ. Shruti says, " Âtmâ exists in the hearts of creatures"; " Him who is seen with difficulty, is hidden, exists entered into things, is seated in buddhi, exists in the cave (4), is ancient (5)"; " The one controller, the Âtmâ in all beings"; "The Âtmâ who is in all things "; and so forth. Smriti also says, " Îshvara, O

---

(1) Brahmamayî.　　　　　　　(2) Chidrûpinî.
(3) Kriyâtmaka. Prâna is the vital air, and constant activity in respiration, circulation of blood and so forth are what gives it the vital character. Hence it is said to be activity itself.
4) The cave is the body full of troubles.　　　　(5) Eternal.

6. He, who sees all beings in Âtmâ and Âtmâ in all beings, does not therefor speak ill.

7. In whom all beings have become Âtmâ, what delusion, what grief can there be in that (Âtmâ) of the wiseman who sees oneness?

Arjuna, resides in the hearts of all beings." *It is outside all this*, that is, Brahma is outside all things of the world as the object of enjoyment (1). The Mundaka Upanishat also shows the contradictory characteristics of Brahma : "It is great, divine and unthinkable. It also appears subtler than the subtle. It is more distant than the distant. It also exists near within the body. To those who can see, It resides in the heart."

6. After speaking of the existence of Brahma within and outside all the world, the Upanishat proceeds to explain how men who are liberated in life, are united with Âtmâ and know Brahma, see Âtmâ everywhere. *He*, the knower of Brahma, *who sees all beings*, that is, all things of the world which are parinâmas of Mâyâ, *in Âtmâ* (âtmani), that is, as Âtmâ. That is, he who perceives that the Brahma Which exists in him as conscious Âtmâ also exists as all the things of the world in the aspect of Mâyâ. He who sees *Âtmâ in all beings*, that is, who perceives that the Âtmâ Who is in him is also the Âtmâ in all things, like space in the cup, the curtain and so forth. Just as the distinctions of cup, curtain and so forth do not in reality make any distinction in the space in them, so distinctions of things do not make any distinction in Âtmâ. He who perceives this *does not therefor*, that is, in consequence of this monistic perception, *speak ill*, because Âtmâ is the seat of supreme love. It is because Jivas fail to perceive the One Âtmâ in all things that failure to get happiness always and everywhere induces them to speak ill of things. Shruti says, " The one controller, the Âtmâ in all beings, who makes one form into many. Perpetual happiness comes to the peaceful men who see Him in themselves and not to others " ; " He who knows the Bliss of Brahma (2) is not afraid of anything" ; and so forth. Smriti also says, " As the mighty air, moving everywhere, is seated in space, so know that all beings are seated in Me " ; " He whose self is in Yoga (3), sees Âtmâ in all beings and all beings in Âtmâ. He sees the same everywhere " ; " Supreme joy comes to this Yogî whose mind is peaceful, whose troubles have ceased, who is sinless and has become Brahma" ; and so forth.

7. This Mantra repeats the purport of the preceding Mantra for clearly stating the absence of delusion and grief in him who sees nonduality. *In whom* (yasmin), that is, in which Âtmâ, *all beings have become Âtmâ*, that is, he who perceives all beings to be the One Principle, Atmâ. Grief and delusion caused by attachment, hatred and so forth are

(1) Everything is here conceived to have an inside and an outside. In fact, the thing itself consists of this inside and outside. The inside is Âtmâ and the outside the object of enjoyment (bhogya).

(2) The Bliss of Brahma means the Bliss which is Brahma. Bliss and Brahma are one and not two different things.

(3) That is, whose mind has attained samâdhi.

8. He encompassed the white, bodiless, painless, nerveless, pure and sinless. The Svayambhû, Who is omniscient, rules the mind and is omnipresent, properly distributed the desires among the eternal years.

---

possible only in those who do not know Âtmâ and perceive that many things exist, and not in those who know Âtmâ, are devoid of dualism and have a pure mind, free from desires. The Katha Upanishat says, " There is nothing manifold here. He who sees as if there is manifold existence here gets death after death," and this clearly indicates that only ignorant men, who see manifold existence, that return to sangsâra again and again on account of their being subject to grief and delusion. Those, however, who perceive the Monistic Principle are, on account of their being free from them, liberated from the wheel of sangsâra. Shruti says, " Just as pure water being poured into pure water becomes the same,' so, O Gautama, becomes the Âtmâ of the Muni (1) who knows " ; "It is Âtmâ. He who knows this himself enters into Âtmâ " .; and so forth. Shruti also says, " If the person knows Âtmâ as ' This I am', for which desire and for whose purpose should he trouble his Âtmâ with the troubles of the body ? " " By knowing Him who is seen with difficulty, is hidden, exists entered into things, is seated in buddhi, exists in the cave and is ancient (2) and shining, by means of spiritual Yoga, the peaceful man forsakes joy and grief " ; and so forth.

8. After speaking of the world as Âtmâ and of the greatness of this knowledge, the Upanishat proceeds in this Mantra to show the saguna character of that Âtmâ as body, Jiva and Îshvara and the nirguna character as the Kûtastha. *He*, Âtmâ, becoming Saguna, *encompassed* in the forms of body and Jiva. Encompassed whom ? The *white* (shukra), that is, what is free from the dirt of Rajas and Tamas, shining. In the word *nerveless*, nerve stands for all instruments of work. Hence the word means inactive. *Sinless*, that is, devoid of the sangskáras of dharma and adharma. Shruti says, " The Purusha is shining, formless, existent with inner and outer objects, unborn, prânaless, mindless, white, supreme beyond what is supreme and undecaying (3)." These are the Svarûpa or primary characteristics of Brahma, indicative of Its Nishkala (4) aspect. The Mândûkya Upanishat says the same thing in determining the Fourth (5) State of Âtmâ, as, "The Fourth is considered to be He Who is unseeable, unusable, untakeable, undefinable, unthinkable, unspeakable, Whose existence is proved by the perception of one Âtmâ in all conditions (6), in Whom all prapancha (7) ceases, Who is unchangeable, auspicious and non-dual." Nirguna Âtmâ Who is pure Chit (8) is encompassed by Saguna Âtmâ by means of three bodies characterised by wakefulness, dream and sleep. Inspite of being thus encompassed the Âtmâ is really bodiless ; for, although He presides over bodies it is not possible for Him, on

---

(1) Muni means the meditative man.   (2) Vide *ante*, commentary on Mantra 5.
(3) "What is supreme and undecaying" is Prakriti which is supreme beyond its effects Nirguna Brahma is supreme beyond Prakriti out of which all Vikritis arise.
(4) Nishkala is unconnected with Kalâ or Prakriti.   (5) Chaturtha or Turiya.
(6) The conditions of wakefulness, dream and sleep.   (7) The phenomenal world.
(8) Consciousness.

account of His having no connection with gunas, to be endowed with the characteristics of bodies. The Chhândogyopanishat says, " O Maghavan, this body is mortal, in the grasp of death ; it is the seat of this immortal bodiless Âtmâ. Good and evil influence him who has a body. Good and evil do not forsake a thing which has a body. But good and evil do not touch that which has no body." The meaning is that Âtmâ as Nirguna Kûtastha is bodiless and as Saguna Jîva is possessed of body. The pure consciousness of Saguna Âtmâ is more or less suppressed by the gunas in Himself and thus He becomes a Jiva and a body. Nirguna Kûtastha Âtmâ is encompassed by these Jîva and body aspects of Saguna Âtmâ. It is the opinion of all Upanishats that only one Principle exists and nothing else. This principle is Brahma which is consciousness. Hence the whole world is consciousness. In creation this consciousness appears in every body both in perfection and in imperfection. In perfection it is Kûtastha and in imperfection it is Jiva and body. How does perfect consciousness become imperfect ? Because of its unbeginning Creative Shakti (1), possessed as it is of inscrutable Shaktis. Is this Shakti consciousness or something different from consciousness ? She (2) is consciousness on account of there being actually no difference between a Shakti and the possessor of a Shakti. How does Creative Shakti who is consciousness take away (3) consciousness ? We have said, because Brahma is possessed of inscrutable Shaktis. The Aitareya Upanishat also says, " This heart (4) and mind, this consciousness, Îshvarahood, scientific knowledge, true knowledge (5), intelligence, sight, sustenance, thinking, talent, sorrowfulness, remembrance, determination, perseverence, vitality, desire, dominance —all these are the names of true knowledge. This is Brahma, this is Indra ; this is Prajâpati. All these Devas, these five Mahâbhûtas, namely, earth, air, space, water and fire, and those small and other creatures ; the causes and the rest, namely, those born of eggs, those born of the womb, those born of moisture and those springing out of the soil— horses, kine, men, elephants, whatever living animals walk or fly and whatever is immovable— all this derives its existence from knowledge, is established in knowledge. The world is derived from knowledge, established in knowledge. Knowledge is Brahma." It is owing to the Karmik impressions of Jîvas consisting of desires for enjoyment that the phenomenal world (6) appears in Vyâvahâra as unconscious. Under the influence of impressions Jîvas desire enjoyment, and the phenomenal world of enjoyment appears for the satisfaction of these desires. It is owing to the imperfect consciousness of Jîvas that they desire enjoyment and regard the phenomenal world as unconscious and enjoyable. Hence impressions are the cause of Jivas' imperfect consciousness. The impressions are composed of gunas and evolved (7) out of gunas. Mâyâ, the Gunamayî Creative Shakti of Brahma, covers Her own perfect consciousness in the aspect of Karma and Karmic impressions and appears as Jiva and so forth. Shruti says, " The Chhandas (8), Yajnas, Kratus (9), Vratas (10), the past, the future and

---

(1) Srishtishakti.   (2) Srishtishakti.   (3) Literally, reduce.
(4) Heart (hridaya), the seat of buddhi.
(5) Consciousness—Sangjnâna.   Îshvarahood—Âjnâna.
    Scientific knowledge—Vijnâna.   True knowledge—Prajnâna.
(6) Phenomenal world—prapancha.   (7) Parinâma.   (8) Chhandas—Vedas.
(9) Kratus are a class of yajnas.   (10) Vratas are vows such a Chândrâyana.

all that (5) the Vedas speak of, as Mâyî (6) creates this universe, the other is bound to it by Mâyâ ; know Mâyâ to be Prakriti and Mâyî to be Maheshvara (7). It is by His limbs (8) that all this world is pervaded" ; and so forth. This is Brahma's creative play. " He desired I shall become many for creation. He performed tapas. Performing tapas He created all this, everything that is in the world. Creating it He entered into it." This Shruti proves that the creation is derived from desire, that is, karmik - impression, and tapas, that is, knowledge. Hence there are two aspects of Mâyâ, who may also be called Creative Shakti, Mûlaprakriti or Saguna Brahma, namely, the aspect of desire and the aspect of knowledge. In the aspect of desire She is composed of the three gunas and in the aspect of knowledge She is consciousness. As composed of the three gunas, She is the cause of the gross, subtle and causal bodies and, as consciousness, She is the cause of all sensations and perceptions in the bodies. The three gunas also are not different from consciousness. In dissolution they exist in the form of Brahma. Shruti says, " Then (9) the One (10) lived windless (11), united with Prakriti. Nothing existed besides It " ; " O good one, this world existed before as existence, one and without a second " ; and so forth. At the end of dissolution also the gunas exist as consciousness, in a state of equilibrium, as the self of Îshvara (12), for which Îshvara is possessed of the qualities of omniscience, rulership and so forth. Shruti says, " They (the Yogîs) saw the Shakti who is the Deva (13), hidden by Her own gunas," that is, the primary aspect of Creative Shakti in which She is perfect Brahma-consciousness is hidden when She appears as the three gunas. For the purpose of creation this Bhagavatî Shakti forsakes, in part, the state of equilibrium and homogeneity (14), and becomes heterogeneous as three gunas by virtue of Her possessing inscrutable powers. Hence the world, in which She, again, enjoys as Jîva owing to Her connection with the gunas in inequilibrium and rules everything as Îshvara owing to Her connection with the gunas in equilibrium. Never do the gunas exist separated from consciousness, because consciousness is all-pervading. Hence the theory of their being different from consciousness becomes untenable, as also for the reason that at the end of dissolution they appear out of Brahma, Which is consciousness, and, again, at dissolution merge into It. Shruti says, " This Supreme Brahma is sung. In It the three are well-established. It is also Akshara." The three are object of enjoyment, enjoyer and director (15), and Akshara, that is, the Undecaying One, is Nirguna Brahma. After speaking of the encompassing character of Saguna Âtmâ as body and as Jîva, the Mantra proceeds to speak of Him as Director. *Svayambhû*, that is, He who becomes Himself, causeless. By virtue of His being possessed of inscrutable powers He Himself appears as Îshvara and as the world. *Omniscient*, that is, He who sees everything..

(5) The present is included in this "all that".   (6) Mâyî—possessor of Mâyâ.
(7) Maheshvara—Supreme Îshvara.   The highest creator.
(8) Limbs—avayava, parts.   Although Maheshvara is impartible, parts are attributed to Him in the analogy of diversities in the world.
(9) Then—in dissolution.   (10) One—Brahma or Purusha.
(11) Windless—breathless.   Brahma-existence does not require breathing.   Breathing is a physical characteristic, dependent on the existence of air and the body.   In dissolution, however, nothing exists save Brahma-existence
(12) Îshvarâtmanâ.   (13) The Deva here is Shining Brahma.   (14) Ekarasatva.
(15) Director—prerayitâ or niyantâ : He who directs and controls all enjoyment.

9. Into blinding darkness they enter who practise avidyâ. Into even greater darkness they who are attached to vidyâ.

This indicates that He presides over the causal body. *Rules the mind* —this indicates that He presides over the subtle body. *Omnipresent*, that is, exists on all sides. The original is *paribhû*. It may also mean, exists above (pari—upari) all things. This indicates that He presides over the gross body also. (2)

Properly (Yâthâtathyatah), that is, as it should be. *Desires* (arthân), that is, impressions of Karma performed for welfare in the next world. *Years* stand for time. *Eternal years* means eternal time. Time is thus spoken to be eternal. The Prashnopanishat says, "The year is Prajâpati. He has two paths, southern and northern. Those who perform Yajnas and so forth attain the Lunar Loka. These return again. Hence these rishis who desire progeny go to the south(3). And those who seek Âtmâ by brahmacharyya (4 , faith(5) and vidyâ (6) go to the Sun by the northern path(7)." Here also Shruti places the Karmas of men in Prajâpati who personates the year, month, day and night.

9. This and the following Mantras explain the varieties of those Karmas and where they are respectively placed. Karma for the next world is of two kinds, namely, that which causes return to this world and that which gives immortality. The wiseman who knows Brahma and perceives non-duality, or "who sees all beings in Âtmâ and Âtmâ in all beings" and "in whom all beings have become Âtmâ," there is nothing he has got to do. for he has no necessity and no hankering for the next world. He becomes liberated even in this world and even if he does Karma it does not bind him. This has been said in the Second Mantra. Shruti says, "When all the desires resting in his heart are removed, then the mortal becomes immortal and tastes of Brahma here" ; "When the seer(8) sees the shining Purusha who is the doer, lord and source of Brahmâ, then the wiseman is washed of virtue and sin and, spotless, attains supreme equanimity" ; "He is the best of Brahma-knowers who sports in Âtmâ and does (similar) (9) work" ; "The desires of him whose desires have been gratified (10) and who has known Âtmâ all disappear even here (11)" ; " Those who are devoted to Brahma are merged in Brahma and freed from birth" ; and so forth. Smriti also says, "But the man who rejoices in Âtmâ, is satisfied with Âtmâ, and is content in Âtmâ, for him there is nothing to do. For him there is no interest in things done in this world, nor any in things not done, nor does any object of his depend on any being" ; and so forth. But every one is not entitled (12) to knowledge of Brahma, Which is eternal, pure, enlightened and liberated. Attachment (13) to Brahma is for wisemen (14) alone. The ignorant are attached to Karma. So long as the mind is not purified, there can not be perfection of knowledge.

---

(2) The three aspects of Íshvara in which He presides over the causal body, subtle body and gross body are called Ísha, Sútra or Hiranyagarbha, and Virât or Vaishvânara.
(3) The Pitriyâna.   (4) Celibacy and all-round physical and mental purity.
(5) Shraddhâ.   (6) Devatâjnâna, the knowledge that Prajâpati is Âtmâ.
(7) The Devayâna.   (8) Jiva.
(9) Similar work is meditation, cultivation of knowledge, vairâyga (dispassion) and so forth.
(10) That is, who has no more desires.
(11) In this life.   (12) Adhikârî.   (13) Nishthâ.   (14) Jnâni.

The mind is not purified so long as there is not an end of desires. Desires cannot cease so long as Nishkâma (1) Karma is not practised. Hence ignorant men who seek liberation should by all means practise Nishkâma Karma. Such ignorant men, however, as are thoroughly deluded and seek the happiness of a life in Heaven, perform the Karmas prescribed in Shruti and Smriti with a craving for their fruits and thus abide in ignorance(2). Their desires do not cease and their Sangsâra(3) does not end. Shruti says, " The boys(4) who live in ignorance in various ways, think that their purpose has been fulfilled(5). Men who are devoted to Karma do not know (Âtmâ) through attachment. Hence their life in Heaven end and stricken by grief they then fall" ; " The deluded men who consider yajnas and works of public utility as the best and do not know of any thing better, they enjoy on the surface of Heaven earned by their good deeds and thereafter enter into this or even a worse loka ; " and so forth. Smriti also says, " Enveloped is knowledge by this constant enemy· of the wise in the form of desire which is, O Kaunteya (6), insatiable like fire" ; " The knowers of the three(7), the Soma-drinkers, the purified from sin, worshipping Me with sacrifice, pray for life in Heaven. They, ascending to the holy loka of the Lord of Suras (8 , enjoy in Heaven the pleasures of Devas. They, having enjoyed the spacious loka of Heaven, their virtues exhausted, enter into the mortal loka. Thus following the Dharma enjoined by the three, desiring desires, they get birth and death" ; and so forth. The ignorant men, however, whose minds being enlightened by Guru or Shâstra, consider Heavenly happiness to be small, and, knowing Brahma to be bliss, wish for a permanent cessation of the sorrows of Sangsâra, and, thinking the Devas worshipped in various Karmas to be Brahma Itself, perform the duties of their castes and âshramas (9), they attain Brahma-loka(10) and become immortal. Hence there are two classes of men who are entitled to liberation, namely, those who are wise 11) and those who perform nishkâma Karma. Wisemen, who know the true aspect of Âtmâ, are established in liberation in llfe and, making happiness and sorrow the same(12), rejoice in Âtmâ and, in fact, live in Âtmâ. Leaving this world (13) they are liberated from body and merged in Brahma Which is consciousness. Although performers of nishkâma Karma do not realise the true aspect(14) of Brahma in Âtmâ, they perceive that all forms of happiness end in sorrow. They thus acquire Apara Vairâgya(15), characterised by a dislike for all objects visible and known from Shruti(16),

---

(1) Selfless ; with no purpose.   (2) Avidyâ.
(3) Physical existence subject to birth and death.
(4) The word is indicative of foolish existence.
(5) That is, there is nothing beyond Karma. to which they are attached.
(6) Son of Kunti, Arjuna.   (7) The three, that is, three Vedas.
(8) The Lord of Suras is Indra.
(9) The âshramas, or stations of life, are four, namely, Brahmacharyya, Gârhasthya, Vânaprastha and Sannyâsa. Brahmacharyya âshrama is celibate boyhood in which the boy receives education in his preceptor's house. Gârhasthya âshrama is the station of family life up to the age of fifty. Vânaprastha âshrama is hermitage in the woods after the age of fifty. Sannyâsa Ashrama is the state of total renunciation of the world.
(10) Brahmaloka is the loka of Brahmâ.   (11) Jnâni.
(12) That is, having equal disregard for happiness and sorrow.
(13) That is, when they die.   (14) Svarûpa.
(15) Inferior Dispassion. See Pâtanjala Darshana.
(16) Objects known from Shrûti are heavenly objects to be acquired by Yajnas.

and having recourse to Yoga they reach the path of gradual liberation by nishkâma Karma. There in the Satya-loka(1), their minds being purified, they acquire Para Vairâgya(2), characterised by an equal view of happiness and sorrow, and a realisation of the monistic Brahma Principle and are liberated at the end of the Kalpa. Bhagavân Vâsudeva(3 says, " For a Muni who is seeking Yoga, Karma is said to be the means. For him when he is enthroned in Yoga, cessation from Karma is said to be the means" ; " White and black, these are thought to be the world's everlasting paths. By the one he goes who returns not, by the other he who returns again. Knowing these paths, O Pârtha, no Yogî is deluded. Hence, O Arjuna, be fixed in Yoga in all times. The fruit of meritorious deeds, attached to the study of the Vedas, to Yajnas, to austerities and to charities, the Yogî surpasses them all by knowing this and goes to the first and supreme place(4)" ; and so forth. Shruti and Smriti also say, " The peaceful men who, living on alms in forests, practise tapas and shraddhâ, and wise men become taintless and by the solar gate go where lives the immortal Purusha of undecaying self " (5 ; " When dissolution comes at the end of the life of Brahmâ, all of them (6) along with Brahmâ, having attained Âtmâ, inter into the supreme state" ; and so forth. They are wise men in comparison with those who consider yajnas and other Karma as the best, and not for having attained knowledge of monistic Brahma. Now, what is the necessity for such men as can perform nishkâma Karma to perform Karma at all ? It is but reasonable that those who forsake fruits of Karma should forsake Karma as well and not perform Karma which, even if performed without desire for its fruits, will grant fruit to its performer in the shape of life in Brahma-loka by virtue of his knowledge(7) that it bears such fruit. There is the neceessity on account of their minds being impure and for want of realisation of Brahma. So long as the mind is impure and so long as Brahma is not realised, cessation of Karma (8) is not possible. Control (9) of the organs of action also does not bring about cessation of Karma owing to the restlessness of the mind, the impossibility of resting in Paramâtmâ, and the touch with objects. Such a mind is bound to do Karma and hence it is useless controlling the organs of action. Bhagavân(10) also has blamed forsaking of Karma. He has said, " Who sits controlling the organs of action, but dwelling in his mind on the obects of the senses, that deluded man is called a hypocrite" ; "Perform you prescribed action, for action is better than inaction" ; " Mayst thou not have attachment to inaction" ; and so forth. In fact, those whose proper sphere(11) is Karma simply increase their mental impurity by forsaking it, for then the mind, freed from the activity of the organs of action, freely dwells on objects. It may be said, let their minds rest in vichâra (12) of the true aspect of Brahma. But that is not possible, because such vichâra can not take place in an impure mind. It is when the light of

(1) The highest of the Seven Lokas, the seat of Brahmâ or Hiranyagarbha.
(2) Superior Dispassion. See Pâtanjala Darshana
(3) Shrîkrishna in the Gîtâ.
(4) Brahmahood First, because Brahma is the cause (kârana) of the world.
(5) Vide ante—Commentary on Mantra 3.
(6) Performers of nishkâma Karma whose minds have been thoroughly purified in Satya-loka and who have consequently attained perfect Brahmajnâna.
(7) This knowledge is derived from Shâstra.
(8) Naishkarmmya.   (9) Nigraha.   (10) Shrîkrishna in the Gîtâ.
(11) Adhikâra.   (12) Discursive contemplation.

10.   Different is said to be by vidyâ and different by avidyâ. This we have heard of peaceful men who have explained it to us.

11.   Vidyâ and avidyâ, he who knows these both together, by avidyâ he surpasses death and by vidyâ tastes of immortality.

Brahma shines on the purified mind then that wiseman, who is liberated in life, lives by vichâra. The proper sphere of others whose minds are impure is Karma. Shruti says, " These are distant from and contradictory to each other, avidyâ(1) and what is known as vidyâ (2)." Here the term *vidyâ* means realisation of Brahma and not merely Devatâjnâna(3), because a combination of Devatâjnâna and avidyâ is possible. And this Karma purifies ₎the mind when performed without desire for fruits, with resignation to Îshvara and with Devatâjnâna. Those' who can fortunately acquire this purification in this life rise to the state of knowledge and enter into Brahmahood beyond all lokas. Those, however, who are not so fortunate attain Brahmaloka and there in course of time their minds are purified and they are established in knowledge.

Into blinding darkness (andhang tamas), that is, into the Pitriyâna path beginning in smoke and distitute of the light of Âtmâ, *they enter who practise avidyâ.* *Avidyâ* means ignorance, that is, pure Karma opposed to knowledge of Atmâ, sakâma (performed with desire for fruits) and destitute of Devatâjnâna. Shruti says, "These (4) who perform Yajnas and works of public utility and charities in villages get unto the smoke, from the smoke unto the night, from the night unto the other (5) fortnight, from the other fortnight unto the six months in which the sun travels south. They do not get unto the year. From the six months they attain the Pitriloka" ; and so on. *Into even greater darkness they* enter *who are attached to vidyâ*, that is, to Devatâjnâna, to Panchâgnividyâ (6), to Devatâs with the knowledge that they are Brahma. They are attached to vidyâ but have forsaken Karma. The idea is that the fate of forsakers of Karma in the Pitriyâna path is darker than that of performers of Karma.

10.   Such are the different fruits of vidyâ and avidyâ when practised separately, and the following Mantra (7) speaks of their different fruits when they are practised together. *Of peaceful men* (dhîrânâng) that is, from learned men, âchâryyas, *who have explained it,* that is, the subject of vidyâ and avidyâ, *to us.*

11.   Great is the effect of the practice of vidyâ and avidyâ together. This Mantra says what parts they separately contribute to produce this effect. *Vidyâ* is Devatâjnâna and *avidyâ* is Karma. *He who knows,* that is, practises, *these both together*, that is, practises avidyâ enlightened by vidyâ. Karma accompained by Devatâjnâna becomes free from the desire to enjoy heavenly happiness and is, consequently, nishkâma. Such being the case, *by avidyâ*, that is, by Karma, *he*, the performer of such nishkâma Karma, *surpasses death.* Death here stands for the

---

(1) Karma, ajnâna.   (2) Jnâna
(3) The general knowledge that the Devatâ worshipped is Brahma, that is, it is Brahma Which appears in the form of the different Devatâs whom people worship.
(4) Householders.   (5) Dark.
(6) The science of Five Fires explained in the Fifth Chapter of the Chhândogyopanishat. The five fires are the firmament, cloud, earth, male and female. A Jiva's Karma makes him travel through these in the cycle of his reincarnation   (7) Mantra 11.

12. Into blinding darkness they enter who worship asambhûti. Into even greater darkness they who are attached to sambhûti.

13. Different is said to be from sambhava and different from asambhava. This we have heard of peaceful men who have explained it to us.

14. Sambhûti and vinâsha, he who knows these both together, by vinâsha he surpasses death and by sambhûti tastes of immortality.

---

cycle of birth and death. By Karma he attains purification of mind and, through cessation of desire for enjoyment, becomes liberated from connection with the gross body which is the seat of enjoyment. And *by vidyâ*, that is, by Devatâjnâna and by Brahmajnâna (1) which is its perfection, *tastes of*, that is, attains to, *immortality*, that is, Brahmaloka characterised by non-return to the mortal world and liberation at the termination of the Kalpa. Shruti says, "Those who know this (2) and those who, living in the forest, practise shraddhâ and tapas, they get unto the light, from the light unto the day, from the day unto the waxing (3) fortnight, from the waxing fortnight unto the six months in which the sun moves in the north, from the months unto the year, from the year unto the sun, from the sun unto the moon, from the moon unto the lightning. Thence that Purusha, who is not a man, takes him to Brahma (4). This is the Devayâna Path."

12. The above purpose is again set forth in this and the two following Mantras, with reference to the worship of the effect (Kâryya) and the cause (Kârana). *Sambhûti* is the cause of the world, that is, Saguna Brahma. What *sambhavati* (becomes), that is, appears as the effect, is *sambhûti*. *Asambhûti* is what is not the cause, that is, the effect, the world. In speaking of worship, by *asambhûti* are meant the Devatâs such as Agni, Vâyu and so forth, who identify themselves with the effects. *Into blinding darkness*, that is, the Pitriloka, *they enter who worship asambhûti*, that is, Agni and other Devatâs presiding over effects (Kâryyas), without knowing that they are in reality Îshvara and with desire for fruits. *Into even greater darkness they* enter *who are attached to sambhûti*, that is, to Saguna Brahma or Ishvara who is the cause of the world. Karma being their proper sphere, abandonment of Karma consigns these men, who have no Brahmajnâna, to terribly dark lokas inspite of their Devatâjnâna.

13. *Sambhava* is sambhûti explained above. *From sambhava* means from worship of Saguna Brahma. *From asambhava* means from asambhûti, that is, from worship of Agni and other Devatâs presiding over effects. The rest is as before (Mantra 10).

14. *Sambhûti* is Saguna Brahma. *Vinâsha* means destruction, here that which is destroyed, namely, Agni and other Devatâs presiding over effects. Destruction is identified with what is destroyed because there is no difference between a quality and its possessor (5).

---

(1) Realisation of Brahma.   (2) This, that is, Panchâgnividyâ. *Vide ante.*
(3) Waxing, that is, bright.   (4) Brahma, that is, Brahmaloka.
(5) Quality—Dharma. Its possessor—Dharmî.
     It is the same principle as that Shakti and the possessor of Shakti are the same.

3

15. By a golden vessel is the face of Truth covered. Do Thou, O Pûshâ, uncover it for him who is devoted to Truth, for sight.

16. O Pûshâ, Ekarshi, Yama, Sûryya, Prâjâpatya, remove the rays, withhold the tejas. Let me see that aspect of Thine which is the most beneficial. He who is that Purusha, He I am.

---

15. After speaking of the immortality of those who combine vidyâ with avidyâ or sambhûti with asambhûti, the Upanishat proceeds, in the guise of a prayer at the time of death, to show by what path that immortality is attained. This is done by these last four Mantras. *By a golden vessel,* that is, by the bright solar orb, *is the face,* that is, the aspect, *of Truth,* that is, that is, Brahma (1) covered. Shruti says, " And the name of that Brahma is Truth". Shruti also says, " And this Golden Purusha who is seen within the sun, golden-bearded, golden-haired, golden all over from the toe-nails." The sense is that the aspect of Brahma, the Purusha (2) in the sun, is hidden from the sight of men by the shining orb. Shruti says, " The command is, the sun is Brahma." *Do thou, O Pûshâ,* who is the *poshaka,* or supporter of Jîvas, by the dispensation of fruits of Karma, *uncover it,* that is, the face or aspect of Brahma. When Jivas rise from the gross body (3), Deva Pûshâ thereupon leads them to the paths they deserve by their Karma. Shruti says, " O Pûshâ, Lord of Path, we invite Thee to us, like a chariot, for work and gain of food" ; " O powerful one, clear the paths for gain of food, conquer the obstructors, give fruition to our works " ; " Be the charioteer (4) of our Yajna" ; " O master of food, thou maintainest all mâyâs (5). O Pûshâ, may thy gifts here be beneficial" ; and so forth. *For him,* that is, for me. *For sight* (drishtaye), that is, for seeing the Purusha in the sun who is Truth. This Mantra says that those who are devoted to truth attain the Purusha in the sun. From the sun they go to Brahmaloka. Shruti says " He becomes established in the sun full of tejas (6). As a snake is freed from its skin, so is he freed from sin and carried up to Brahmaloka by Sâmas (7). He sees the Purusha (8) who is superior to this Aggregate Jîva (9) and resides in every body."

16. This Mantra speaks of Deva Pûshâ as the dispenser of the fruits of Karma and the possessor of the qualities of rulership and soforth of the world. *O Pûshâ,* that is, maintainer of the world. *O Ekarshi,* that is, he who goes alone. There is none other in whose company or with whose help he guides Jîvas to their respective paths. Or, he is the fire called by the name Ekarshi. Shruti says, " The faithful shrotriyas (10) who perform their duties (11), are faithful to Brahma (12) and themselves

---

(1) Saguna Brahma.
(2) Person, the deity or consciousness which is the soul of the sun and presides over it.
(3) That is, die.   (4) That is, lead our religious works as a charioteer leads a chariot.
(5) Sâyana explains mâyâ here as prajnâ, knowledge.   (6) Light.
(7) The Sâmaveda which represents three parts of Om.
(8) Paramâtmâ.   (9) Jîvaghana, Hiranyagarbha.
(10) Shrotriyas are those who have studied Shruti or Veda.
(11) The duties of their caste and Âshrama.
(12) Brahma here is Apara Brahma or Hiranyagarbha.

17. Now may the air become immortal air and this body reduced to ashes. Om, O kratu, remember, remember deeds ; O kratu, remember, remember deeds.

18. O Agni, lead me to wealth by the good path, knowing, O Deva, all my deeds. Remove from me deceitful sin. I offer thee an abundance of words of obeisance.

offer obtations to Ekarshi." And this fire, appearing as the deity presiding over the path, leads the hotâ (1) to Brahmaloka earned by him. O *Yama*, that is, he who controls the fruits of Jîvas' Karma. O *Sûryya*— it is because Pûshâ leads Jîvas to their respective lokas according to the desire of the Sûryya-devatâ called Âditya that he is glorified by the name Sûryya. Or, Sûryya (sun , who is the source (2) of the world, appears as Devatâ Pûshâ to place Jîvas in their places according to their respective Karma, and hence Pûshâ is Sûryya. Shruti says, "O Pûshâ, the golden boats (3) of thine which move in the sea, in the firmament, by them thou goest in mission at the will of Sûryya." O *Prâjâpatya*, that is, son of Prajâpati, so called because he maintains prajâ or people by making them come by the fruits of their Karma. The Sanghitâ Shruti (4) also says, " Son of Vimuch "—Vimuch is Prajâpati. *Withhold the tejas*, that is, the scorching aspect of Deva Âditya. *Let me see*, that is, so ordain that I may see, *that aspect of Thine which is the most beneficial*, that is, which is the seat of supreme good. Shruti says, " One is thy white, another is thy black—like dyau (6) thou hast these two aspects, day and night." *He who is that Purusha, He I am*—the supplicant's Devatâjnâna is shown hereby. *He who is that Purusha*, that is, the Âditya Purusha in the solar orb, *He I am*, and hence I pray to be united with him. Shruti says, ' The Purusha who is seen in the sun, He I am, verily He I am."

. 17. The prayer to Pûshâ ended, the man on feeling his prâna about to leave the body remembers the Karma, or work, which he has performed since birth and which will determine his path in the next world. *Now*, at the time of death, *may the air*, which is the prâna in my gross body, leave it and, *become immortal air*, that is, remain for ever as the prâna in the subtle body without ever again getting into a gross body. *And may this body become reduced to ashes* after death. *Om* is the symbol (pratîka) of Brahma, the Pranava which being the self of Truth should be uttered at the inception of every purpose. *O kratu— kratu* is sangkalpa. that is, purpose. The dying man addresses himself as kratu or purpose, because purposes being the cause of the Jivahood of Jîvas, Jîvas may be said to be made of them. *Remember deeds*, that is, work done. Shruti says, " And verily the Purusha is made of purpose. As his purpose in this world is so he becomes after death." The repetition is for emphasis.

18. In this Mantra the dying man prays again. *O Agni*, the Devatâ presiding over fire, to whom I have offered oblations from my birth with the knowledge that thou art Îshvara. *Lead me to wealth*, that is, to

---

(1) Hotâ is he who performs homa.
(2) Source—Savitâ.
(3) Compare the golden boat of Charon.
(4) Rigveda Sanghitâ.
(5) Dyau—Sky or the Sun.

the attainment of the fruits of Karma, *by the good path*, that is, Devayâna Path, from which there is no return again. *Deceitful sin* is sin that
prevents immortality. *I offer thee an abundance of words of obeisance*,
that is, I bow to thee again and again, lead me by the Devayâna Path
to Brahmaloka which is immortality. .

The concluding commentary.

In this Upanishat the First Mantra speaks of Brahma as pervading
the world and that, thinking this, no one should crave for enjoyment.
The knower of Âtmâ who, knowing this, performs works with the sense
that Âtmâ is everywhere, is not bound by those works. He becomes
liberated in life and the conflict between Jnâna (knowledge) and Karma
(work) does not arise in his case. This is the purpose of the Second
Mantra. The Third Mantra specifies the faithless, self-destructive men
who are quite opposite of the knowers of Âtmâ, the liberated in life,
and who, for want of a life in the next world, come by, after death,
a most terrible fate as insects, flies and the like. After specifying the
fate of the faithless, the Upanishat, in the Fourth Mantra, speaks shortly
of the two aspects, Saguna and Nirguna, of Âtmâ and of His being
the seat of all Karmas. In the Fifth Mantra the two aspects are more
clearly set forth. The Sixth and Seventh Mantras speak of the Monistic
perception and mental purity of the liberated in life, the knower of
Âtmâ. The Eighth Mantra speaks of the Primary characteristics
of Âtmâ as Kûtastha conciousness and of His Secondary Saguna characteristics when He appears as Jîva, Îshvara and body. The Mantras
from the Ninth to the Fourteenth speak of the two kinds of fate of
the faithful people whose minds are impure and knowledge insufficient.
Among them the Ninth and Twelfth Mantras, beginning with "Into
blinding darkness they enter," speak of the Pitriyâna, characterised by a
return to this world, as the lot of performers of Sakâma Karma and
those who give up Karma without being entitled to give it up. The
Eleventh and Fourteenth Mantras speak of Devayâna, characterised by
non-return to this world, as the lot of performers of Nishkâma Karma
who combine Jnâna with Karma and worship Saguna Brahma. The
Mantras from the Fifteenth to the Eighteenth show, in the guise of the
prayer of a dying man, the Devatâjnâna and knowledge of the true
nature of Âtmâ of him who is entitled to the Devayâna Path.

Here ends the commentary on the Îsha Upanishat of the Vâjasaneya
Sanghitâ by Satyânanda, seeking refuge in the feet of Shri Sadguru (1).
Om Guru.

---

(1) The characteristics of Sadguru are found in the following Mantra of obeisance to Him :—
" I bow to Sadguru who is Brahma-bliss, the grantor of supreme happiness ; who is alone and
knowledge itself ; who is unaffected by pairs of opposities and like unto the sky ; who is the aim
of sayings like 'That Thou art' ; who is one, eternal, dirtless and unmoving ; who is the witness
of all minds ; who is beyond the reach of comprehension and free from the three gunas."

ईशोपनिषत् ।

सत्यानन्दकृतभाष्यसमेता वाजसनेयसंहिताख्यशुक्लयजुर्वेदीया

ईशोपनिषत् ।

सत्यानन्दकृतभाष्यभूमिका ।

ब्रह्मादयं ज्ञानरूपं कर्त्तारं भोक्तारमीशम् ।
सूक्ष्मं स्थूलतमं वन्दे जगत्कारणकारणम् ॥

ईशावास्यमित्याद्यष्टादशमन्त्रविशिष्टायामुपनिषदि निष्कामी मुमुचुरेवा-
धिकारी मुक्ति: प्रयोजनमात्मा विषय आत्मलक्षणप्रतिपादनेन मोक्षोपायनिर्देश:
सम्बन्ध: । आत्मस्वरूपोपलब्धिरेव मुक्ति: । सा चोपलब्धिश्चित्तशुद्धिसापेक्षा ।
चित्तशुद्धिश्च कर्म्मसापेक्षा । येषामात्मस्वरूपोपलब्धिर्जाता ते इहैव मुक्ता:, न
तेषां कर्म्मणि प्रयोजनं न कर्म्मदेष: । ये पुनरविशुद्धचित्तत्वादनात्मविदस्तैश्चित्त-
शुद्धिलाभार्थं निष्कामिणेश्वरार्पणबुद्ध्या कर्म कर्त्तव्यं । इत्थं प्रकारेण कर्म्माणि
कुर्व्वन् येषामिहैव जन्मनि चित्तशुद्धिर्जायते ते जीवन्मुक्ता भवन्ति देहान्ते चात्म-
स्वरूपे विलीयन्ते । निष्कामकर्म्मिणो येषान्तु चित्तकलुषाणीहैव न स्खलन्ति,

ते देहान्ते क्रममुक्तः पन्यानं देवयानं प्राप्नुवन्ति । तत्र ते क्रमेण चित्तशुद्धिं लब्ध्वा ब्रह्मलोके तिष्ठन्त्याकल्पान्तं, कल्पान्ते च ब्रह्मणि विलीयन्ते । सर्व्ववेदान्त-सिद्धान्तसम्मतमेतत् सर्व्वं व्याख्यास्यामो मन्त्रार्थमुखेन ।

———— — —

ईशोपनिषत् ।

शान्तिपाठ: ।

ॐ पूर्णमद: पूर्णमिदं पूर्णात् पूर्णमुदच्यते ।
पूर्णस्य पूर्णमादाय पूर्णमेवावशिष्यते ॥
ॐ शान्ति: शान्ति: शान्ति: ।

*　　　*　　　*　　　*

ईशा वास्यमिदं सर्वं यत् किञ्च जगत्यां जगत् ।
तेन त्यक्तेन भुञ्जीथा मा गृध: कस्यस्विद्धनम् ॥ १ ॥

सत्यानन्दकृतभाष्यम् ।

चिद्रूपेण ब्रह्मणा परिदृश्यमानं क्षयोपचयलक्षणं सर्व्वमेव चराचरं जगत्पदार्थं
आच्छादनीयं तद्भावभावितव्यमित्युच्यते, ईशा वास्यमिति । ईशा ईशिता शास-
यिता जगत: सृष्टिस्थितिनाशकर्त्ता ईश्वरेणेत्यर्थ: । स च ईश्वरश्चैतन्यस्वरूप:
कर्त्तृत्वस्वभावात् । "एष हि द्रष्टा स्रष्टा श्रोता घ्राता रसयिता मन्ता बोद्धा
कर्त्ता विज्ञानात्मा पुरुष: । स परेऽक्षरे आत्मनि सम्प्रतिष्ठते"(१) इति श्रुति: ।
तेनेश्वरेण जगदास्यमाच्छादनीयम् । जगत्पदार्थानां लौकिकदृष्ट्या जगद्रूपत्वे
सत्यपि परमार्थदृष्ट्या तेषां चिद्रूपत्वमवधार्य्यमित्यर्थ: । अनन्ताचिन्त्यशक्तिसम्पन्नस्य
ब्रह्मणो मायाशक्तिरिव जगद्रूपेण विवर्त्तयति । सा च शक्ति: शक्तिशक्तिमतोरभेद-
ल्लाद्ब्रह्माभेदहेतुत्वेन चिद्रूपिणी । सैव सत्त्वरजस्तमोगुणात्मिका जगदुपादानभूता
मूलप्रकृति: । सा शक्तिरात्मनश्चिद्रूपत्वं नियम्य जडरूपेणाभिर्भवति जीवानां

---

(१) प्रश्नोपनिषत् ४।९

कुर्वन्नेवेह कर्माणि जिजीविषेत् शतं समाः ।
एवं त्वयि नान्यथेतोऽस्ति न कर्म लिप्यते नरे ॥ २ ॥

कर्म्मफलभोगसम्पादनार्थं । वस्तुतस्तु जगति न किञ्चिज्जडमस्ति । "सर्वं खल्विदं ब्रह्म"(१), "आत्मैवेदं सर्व" (२), "पुरुष एवेदं विश्वं कर्म्म तपो ब्रह्म परामृतं"(३), "ब्रह्मैवेदममृतं पुरस्ताद्ब्रह्म पश्चाद्ब्रह्म दक्षिणतश्चोत्तरेण । अधश्चोर्ध्वञ्च प्रसृतं ब्रह्मैवेदं विश्वं वरिष्ठम्"(४) इत्यादिश्रुतिवाक्येभ्यः । कर्म्मफलपरिपाकिनः शुद्ध-चित्ता ज्ञानिनः सर्वं जगद्ब्रह्मणाच्छादयन्ति ब्रह्मस्वरूपेण पश्यन्तीत्यर्थः । जगत्यां गतिः परिणामार्थत्वात् परिणामवत्सु पृथिव्यादिलोकेषु यत् किञ्च जगत् परिणामि । तेन तस्मात् सर्व्वेशो जगतो ब्रह्मभावितत्वात् त्यक्तेन त्यक्तं यथा स्यात् तथा फलाकाङ्क्षात्यागेन अनात्मधारणाविवर्जनेन भुञ्जीथाः । कस्यस्वित् निजस्य परस्य वा धनं काम्यवस्तु मा गृधः मा काङ्क्षीरित्यर्थः । खिदिति निपातो निश्चयार्थबोधकः । यदा सर्वं काम्यवस्तु चिद्रूपेण विभाति तदा तस्य काम्य-त्वमेव विनश्यतीति भावार्थः । भगवताप्युक्तं—

"प्रजहाति यदा कामान् सर्वान् पार्थ मनोगतान् ।
आत्मन्येवात्मना तुष्टः स्थितप्रज्ञस्तदोच्यते" इति(५) ॥ १ ॥

कुर्वन्निति । यो नरः एवम्प्रकारेण सर्व्वं ब्रह्मेति ज्ञानसम्पन्नः सन् निष्कामेन फलाभिसन्धिराहित्येन कर्माणीन्द्रियव्यापाराणि कुर्व्वन् इह पृथिव्यां शतं समाः शतसंख्याकान् संवत्सरान् दीर्घायुःपरिमितं कालमपि जिजीविषेत् जीवितु-मिच्छेदिति सम्बन्धः । त्वयि नरे युष्मत्-शब्दव्यवहारेण नरमात्र उपलक्षितः । नान्यथा नान्यः प्रकारः । इत एवम्विधनिष्कामकर्म्मणोऽस्ति येन प्रकारेण कर्म्म न लिप्यते कर्म्मणा न लिप्स्यसे कर्म्मफलं न प्राप्स्यसि । अतात्मज्ञानिनो जीवन्मुक्तावस्था सूचिता । यावद्देहधारणं विद्यते तावन्न कोऽपि ज्ञानी निष्क्रियो जीवेदिन्द्रियादिसम्भवादारब्धकर्म्मवशाच्च । तथाचोक्तं भगवताऽर्जुनं प्रति—

"न हि कश्चित् क्षणमपि जातु तिष्ठत्यकर्म्मकृत् ।
कार्य्यते ह्यवशः कर्म्म सर्व्वः प्रकृतिजैर्गुणैः ॥" इति (६)

(१) छान्दोग्योपनिषत् ३।१४।१

(२) छान्दोग्योपनिषत् ७।२५।२

(३) मुण्डकोपनिषत् २।१।१०

(४) मुण्डकोपनिषत् २।२।१२

(५) भगवद्गीता २।५५

(६) गीता ३।५

असुर्य्या नाम ते लोका अन्धेन तमसावृताः ।
तांस्ते प्रेत्याभिगच्छन्ति ये के चात्महनो जनाः ॥ ३ ॥

ननु ब्रह्मात्मविज्जीवन्मुक्तः प्रकृतिवशादेतद्धर्म्मानुरोधेन लोकसंग्रहार्थं वा
कर्म्माणि कुर्व्वन्नपि सर्व्वत्र ब्रह्मैव पश्यतीत्युक्तमादिमन्त्रेणेशावास्यमित्यादिना ।
काठकेऽप्युक्तं, "पुरमेकादशद्वारमजस्यावक्रचेतसः । अनुष्ठाय न शोचति विमु-
क्तश्च विमुच्यते" इति(१) । स विमुक्त आत्मज्ञानी यदि शतवर्षाण्यपि जिजीविषेत्
तथापि न कर्म्मणा लिप्स्यते । सन् प्रलयो गौरवार्थः बहुतरकर्म्मानुष्ठानेनापि
जीवन्मुक्तस्य न कर्म्मबन्ध इति दर्शयितुं व्यवहृतः । ज्ञानकर्म्मणोर्विरोधोऽज्ञानां
सकामनिष्कामकर्म्मपक्षे न ज्ञानिनामिन्द्रियादिव्यापारमात्रे बोद्धव्यः ।
ज्ञानिनामिन्द्रियादिव्यापारो न तत् कर्म्म यद्बध्नाति जीवं संसारद्रुमे यथा
भगवतो वासुदेवस्य चात्मधर्म्मपालनं । "न मां कर्म्माणि लिम्पन्ति न मे
कर्म्मफले स्पृहा" (२), "आत्मवन्तं न कर्म्माणि निबध्नन्ति धनञ्जय"(३),
"सर्व्वभूतात्मभूतात्मा कुर्व्वन्नपि न लिप्यते"(४) इत्यादि स्मृतिवाक्येभ्यः ।
"भिद्यते हृदयग्रन्थिश्छिद्यन्ते सर्व्वसंशयाः । क्षीयन्ते चास्य कर्म्माणि तस्मिन्
दृष्टे परावरे"(५), "यदा सर्व्वे प्रमुच्यन्ते कामा येऽस्य हृदि स्थिताः ।
अथ मर्त्योऽमृतो भवत्यत्र ब्रह्म समश्नुते"(६), "यदा पश्यः पश्यते रुक्मवर्णं
कर्त्तारमीशं पुरुषं ब्रह्मयोनिम् । तदा विद्वान् पुण्यपापे विधूय निरञ्जनः परमं
साम्यमुपैति" (७) इत्यादिश्रुतिवाक्येभ्यश्च ॥ २ ॥

सम्यगात्मज्ञानलक्षणां जीवन्मुक्तावस्थामुक्त्वा न भाति नास्ति चैतन्य इति सम्यगा-
त्मज्ञानाभावलक्षणां मूढावस्थामाह, असुर्येति । सुरा ज्ञानिनो, न सुरा असुराः
सम्यगात्मज्ञानविहीनाः । "देवासुरा ह वै यत्र संयेतिरे"(८) इत्यादिच्छान्दोग्यो-
पनिषद्दर्शित उपाख्याने "असुराः पाप्मना विविधुः"(८) इत्युक्त्वा तेषामात्मज्यो-
तिर्विरहितं मूढाहङ्काररूपं पापस्वभावं तमःस्वरूपत्वं निर्देशयति । काठकेऽपि,

(१) कठोपनिषत् २।२।१　　　(५) मुण्डकोपनिषत् २।२।८
(२) गीता ४।१४　　　　　　(६) कठोपनिषत् २।२।१४
(३) गीता ४।४१　　　　　　(७) मुण्डकोपनिषत् ३।१।३
(४) गीता ५।७　　　　　　　(८) छान्दोग्योपनिषत् १।२।१
(९) छान्दोग्योपनिषत् १।२।१२-६

"अस्तीति ब्रुवतोऽन्यत्र कथं तदुपलभ्यते"(१), "अस्तीत्येवोपलभ्यस्तत्त्वभावेन चोभयोः । अस्तीत्युपलब्धस्य तत्त्वभावः प्रसीदति"(२), इत्यत्र स्वरूपतटस्थोभय-लक्षणस्य ब्रह्मणोऽस्तित्वमनुपलभ्य नास्तिकः सूचितः । गीताशास्त्रेऽपि, "प्रव-त्तिञ्च निवृत्तिञ्च जना न विदुरासुराः । न शौचं नापि चाचारो न सत्यं तेषु विद्यते । असत्यमप्रतिष्ठन्ते जगदाहुरनीश्वरं । अपरस्परसम्भूतं किमन्यत् कामहेतुकं । एतां दृष्टिमवष्टभ्य नष्टात्मानोऽल्पबुद्धयः । प्रभवन्त्युग्रकर्माणः क्षयाय जगतोऽहिताः"(३) इत्यादि । असुराणां स्वभावापन्ना लोका असुर्य्या नाम लोका असुर्य्य इति नाम्नाभिधानयोग्याः । यद्वा नामशब्दोऽनर्थकः । ते लोका लोक्यन्ते प्राप्यन्ते विशिष्टजन्मान्तररूपाणि कर्म्मफलानि । अन्धेन दृष्टिविरहितेनात्मज्योतिःशून्येन मोक्षस्वरूपेण तमसाऽऽवृता भवन्तीतिशेषः । तां-स्ते प्रेत्य इमं नरदेहं त्यक्त्वा अभिगच्छन्ति प्राप्नुवन्ति । के ते ? ये के चात्म-हनो जनाः । आत्मानं घ्नन्तीत्यात्महनो बुद्धेर्मूढत्वाद्देहातिरिक्तो जरामरणरहितो बोधस्वरूप आत्मा नास्तीतिभावयन्तो नष्टात्मानः । विविधानि हि कर्म्मफलानि भवन्ति । यच्चिन्मयब्रह्मणस्तटस्थसगुणभावस्योपासनरूपं कर्म्म तपस्यादिविधीत-चित्तेनेश्वरार्पणबुद्ध्या श्रद्धया सम्पादितं तदर्च्चिरादिमार्गेण जीवं ब्रह्मलोकं नयति । यतः पुनरावृत्तिर्न विद्यते । ये त्वविशुद्धचित्ताः स्वर्गसुखमेव परमं पुरुषार्थं मन्य-माना स्वदर्थमिष्टापूर्त्तादिकमाचरन्ति सकामेन बुद्ध्या तेषां तत् कर्म्म धूमादि-मार्गेण तान् नयति चन्द्रलोकं यतः पुनरावृत्तिर्भवतीह संसारे । ये पुनर्देहात्म-चिन्तका ऐहिकपरा मूढास्तेषां न काचित् पारलौकिकी गतिर्विद्यतेऽर्च्चिरादिमार्गेण धूमादिमार्गेण वा, परन्तु तेऽविच्छेदेन पुनःपुनरावर्त्तनशीलानि जायस्वक्रियस्वेति-कीटपतङ्गमशकादिक्षुद्रभूतानि भवन्ति । एषां जायस्वम्रियस्वभूतानां लोका असुर्य्या अन्धेन तमसा पूर्ण्माज्ञानेनाऽऽवृताः । "तपःश्रद्धे ये ह्युपवसन्त्यरण्ये शान्ता विद्वांसो भैक्षचर्य्यां चरन्ति । सूर्य्यद्वारेण ते विरजाः प्रयान्ति यत्रामृतः स पुरुषो ह्यव्ययात्मा" (४), "इष्टापूर्त्तं मन्यमाना वरिष्ठं नान्यच्छ्रेयो वेदयन्ते प्रमूढाः । नाकस्य पृष्ठे ते सुकृतेऽनुभूत्वेमं लोकं हीनतरं वा विशन्ति" (५), "अथैतयोः पथोर्न कतरेण च न तानीमानि क्षुद्राण्यसकृदावर्त्तीनि भूतानि भवन्ति जायस्व-

---

(१) कठोपनिषत् २।२।१२   (३) गीता १६।७,८,९

(२) कठोपनिषत् २।२।१३   (४) मुण्डकोपनिषत् १।२।११

              (५) मुण्डकोपनिषत् १।२।१०

अनेजदेकं मनसो जवीयो नैनद्देवा आप्नुवन् पूर्वमर्षत् ।
तद्धावतोऽन्यानत्येति तिष्ठत् तस्मिन्नपो मातरिश्वा दधाति ॥४

क्रियखल्वेत्येतत्तृतीयं स्थानं"(१), "न सम्पराय: प्रतिभाति वालं प्रमाद्यन्तं वित्तमोहेन
मूढं । अयं लोको नास्ति पर इति मानी पुन:पुनर्वश्मापद्यते मे"(२) इत्यादि-
श्रुतिभिः । "शुक्लकृष्णे गती ह्येते जगत: शाश्वते मते । एकया यात्यनावृत्ति-
मन्ययावर्त्तते पुन:"(३), "आसुरीं योनिमापन्ना मूढा जन्मनि जन्मनि । मामप्राप्यैव
कौन्तेय ततो यान्त्यधमां गतिम्" (४) इत्यादिस्मृतिभ्यश्च ॥३॥

पूर्णज्ञानिनो जीवन्मुक्तभावं पूर्णज्ञानिनो जाग्रत्क्रियखोपलक्षितमन्ध-
तामिस्रभावञ्च दर्शयित्वा चिद्रूपिणो ब्रह्मण: खरूपतटस्थावस्थयोर्निर्गुणसगुण-
भावद्वयं दर्शयति, अनेजदिति । अनेजत् एजृकम्पने, अकम्पमानं निश्चलमवस्था-
न्तरविवर्जितं निर्गुणमेकमद्वितीयं सर्वदा सर्वभूतेष्वेकरूपं । शुद्धचिन्मात्रखरूपे
निर्गुणब्रह्मणि न कोऽपि भेद: सम्भवति खगत: सजातीयो विजातीयो वा ।
यदा तु तस्मिन् गुणसम्बन्ध: प्रकटीभवति, तदानन्ताचिन्त्यशक्तिसम्पन्ने परमेश्वरे
खगतभेदा उपजायन्ते तटस्थलक्षणा:, तदुच्यते मनसो जवीय इति । मनसो
मनउपलक्षितान्त:करणाज्जववत्तरं सातिशयेन चञ्चलं परिवर्त्तनशीलञ्च । मन एव
जगत्पदार्थेषु चञ्चलतमं मुहुर्मुहुर्विभिन्नवृत्तिरूपधारणात् । ब्रह्म तु मायारूपं खीकृ-
त्यात्मनि सिद्धचाच्चोभमुत्पाद्य तत्त्चोभमयं निरन्तरपरिवर्त्तनशीलं जगत् सृजति ।
"सोऽकामयत बहु स्यां प्रजायेयेति"(५), "आत्मा वा इदमेक एवाग्र आसीत् ।
नान्यत् किञ्चन मिषत् । स ईक्षत लोकान् नु सृजा"(६), "एतस्माज्जायते
प्राणो मन: सर्वेन्द्रियाणि च । खं वायुर्ज्योतिराप: पृथिवी विश्वस्य धारिणी"(७)
इत्यादिबहुतरश्रुतिवाक्येषु ब्रह्मण: सृष्टिकर्तृत्वं स्रष्टृरूपत्वञ्चोपदिष्टं । सृष्टि-
कर्तृत्वात् स्रष्टृरूपत्वाच्च ब्रह्म मनसोऽपि जववत्तरं । मनो यद्यद्वृत्तिरूपं गृह्णाति
ब्रह्माग्रे तत्तद्वृत्तिरूपेणात्मानं सृजति मनस: संस्कारानुसारेण कर्मफलभोग-
सम्पादनार्थं । नैनद्ब्रह्म देवा द्योतनाद्देवा इन्द्रियाधिष्ठातृदेवगणा आप्नुवन् ।

---

(१) छान्दोग्योपनिषत् ५।१०।८　　　　(४) गीता ८।२६
(२) कठोपनिषत् १।२।६　　　　　　　(५) तैत्तिरीयोपनिषत् २।६
(३) गीता १६।२०　　　　　　　　　(६) ऐतरेयोपनिषत् १।१
(७) मुण्डकोपनिषत् २।१।३

तेषां रजस्तमोमालिन्यात् । श्रुत्यन्तरेऽप्युक्तं, "स वेत्ति वेद्यं न च तस्यास्ति वेत्ता"(१)इति । काठकेऽपि, "पराञ्चि खानि व्यतृणत् स्वयम्भूस्तस्मात् पराङ्पश्यति नान्तरात्मन्" इति (२) । पूर्वमर्षत् मनस इन्द्रियाणाञ्च व्यापारिभ्यः प्रागेव गच्छत् तदर्थमात्मानं सृष्टिकार्यं नियोजयत् । उक्तञ्च काठके, "य एष सुप्तेषु जागर्ति कामं कामं पुरुषो निर्मिमाणः । तदेव शुक्रं तद्ब्रह्म तदेवामृतमुच्यते । तस्मिँल्लोकाः श्रिताः सर्वे तदु नात्येति कश्चन" (३) इति । यदा यतो ब्रह्मैव मन इन्द्रियाणि स्वस्वव्यापारेषु प्रेरयति ततस्तेभ्यः पूर्वमर्षत् गतं प्रेरकस्य प्राक्क्रियावत्त्वात् । तलवकारश्रुतौ, "केनेषितं पतति प्रेषितं मनः केन प्राणः प्रथमः प्रैति युक्तः । केनेषितां वाचमिमां वदन्ति चक्षुः श्रोतं क उ देवो युनक्ति" (४), "श्रोत्रस्य श्रोत्रं मनसो मनो यद् वाचो ह वाचं स उ प्राणस्य प्राणः चक्षुषश्चक्षुः"(५) इत्यादिवाक्यानि ब्रह्मणः सर्वसंवेदनानां मूलस्वरूपत्वं प्रतिपादयन्ति । श्रुत्यन्तरेऽपि, "एष हि द्रष्टा स्प्रष्टा श्रोता घ्राता रसयिता मन्ता बोद्धा कर्ता विज्ञानात्मा पुरुषः । स परेऽक्षर आत्मनि सम्प्रतिष्ठते"(६) इति । ब्रह्मणः सगुणनिर्गुणभेदेन विरुद्धधर्मित्वं प्रस्फुटयितुं पुनराह, तदिति । तद्ब्रह्म धावतः क्रियावतः अन्यान् मनइन्द्रियादीन् अत्येति अतिरिच्य गच्छति । एवं सगुणभावमुक्ता निर्गुणभावमुच्यते तिष्ठत् अचलत् निष्क्रियं अविकारि ब्रह्मतत्त्वम् । अद्वयस्य ब्रह्मणश्चिन्मात्रस्वरूपत्वात् न वस्त्वन्तरस्वरूपप्राप्तिः सम्भवति । परन्तु तस्याचिन्त्यशक्तित्वात् सृष्टौ मायारूपेणाविर्भावः स्यात् । सा ब्रह्ममयी चिद्रूपिणी मायानादिकर्मसंस्कारान् सत्त्वरजस्तमोगुणभावेन स्वात्मनि बिभर्ति । ततः सा चिन्मयी सत्यपि गुणमयी । गुणाश्च चिच्छक्तिरेव द्वितीयत्वाभावात् । पूर्णचिन्मयं ब्रह्म तत्त्रिगुणात्मिका- मायारूपेण जगत्सृष्ट्वा तस्मिन् जीवभावं प्रपद्यते जगल्लीलासिद्धये । "इदं सर्व- मसृजत यदिदं किञ्च । तत् सृष्ट्वा तदेवानुप्राविशत्" (७), "असद्वा इदमग्र आसीत्, ततो वै सदजायत, तदात्मानं स्वयमकुरुत"(८) इत्यादिश्रुतिवाक्यं भ्रः । तस्मिन् ब्रह्मणि अपः कर्माणि धर्माधर्मरूपाणि मातरिश्वा मातरि अन्तरीक्षे श्वयति गच्छतीति मातरिश्वा वायुः प्राणः दधाति धारयति । क्रियात्मकः प्राणः स्वाश्रयाणि कर्माणि ब्रह्मणि स्थापयति तेषां परमार्थतस्तद्रूपत्वात् ॥४॥

(१) श्वेताश्वतरोपनिषत् ३।१९

(२) कठोपनिषत् २।१।१

(३) कठोपनिषत् २।१।१

(४) केनोपनिषत् १।१

(५) केनोपनिषत् १।२

(६) प्रश्नोपनिषत् ४।९

(७) तैत्तिरीयोपनिषत् २।६

(८) तैत्तिरीयोपनिषत् २।७

तदेजति तन्नैजति तद्दूरे तदन्तिके ।
तदन्तरस्य सर्वस्य तदु सर्वस्यास्य वाह्यतः ॥ ५ ॥
यस्तु सर्वाणि भूतानि आत्मन्येवानुपश्यति ।
सर्वभूतेषु चात्मानं ततो न विजुगुप्सते ॥ ६ ॥

ब्रह्मणो निर्गुणसगुणभेदेन विरुद्धधर्मवत्त्वं विस्पष्टयति पूर्व्वमन्त्रार्थं पुनरुक्ता, तदेजतीति । तत् ब्रह्म एजति चलति सक्रियं भवति गुणसम्बन्धात् मायारूपेण । तत् न एजति निष्क्रियं तिष्ठति गुणसम्बन्धाभावात् पूर्णचित्स्वरूपेण । तत् ब्रह्म दूरे निर्गुणस्वरूपेणेन्द्रियैर्मनसा वा अप्राप्यत्वात् । "यतो वाचो निवर्त्तन्ते अप्राप्य मनसा सह"(१) इतिश्रुतेः । तत् उ अन्तिके तदेव ब्रह्म समीपे सगुणभावेन जगन्मयत्वात् । तत् अन्तरभ्यन्तरे चिन्मयात्मरूपेणास्य परिदृश्यमानस्य सर्व्वस्य जगत्पदार्थस्य । "आत्मास्य जन्तोर्निहितो गुहायां"(२), "तं दुर्दर्शं गूढमनुप्रविष्टं गुहाहितं गह्वरेष्ठं पुराणं"(३), "एको वशी सर्वभूतान्तरात्मा"(४), "य आत्मा सर्वान्तरः"(५) इत्यादिश्रुतिभ्यः । "ईश्वरः सर्व्वभूतानां हृद्देशेऽर्जुन तिष्ठति"(६) इतिस्मृतेश्च । तत् उ एव सर्व्वस्यास्य जगत्पदार्थस्य वाह्यतो भोग्यरूपेण । मुख्यक्ष्मुतावपि ब्रह्मणो विरुद्धधर्मवत्त्वं दर्शयति । "ब्रह्मच तद्दिव्यमचिन्त्यरूपं सूक्ष्माच्च तत् सूक्ष्मतरं विभाति । दूरात् सुदूरे तदिहान्तिके च पश्यत्स्विहैव निहितं गुहायाम्"(७) इति ॥५॥

सर्व्वस्यास्य जगतोऽन्तर्व्याह्यतो ब्रह्मणः स्थितिमुक्ता जीवन्मुक्तानामात्मयुक्तानां ब्रह्मविदां सर्व्वात्मत्वदर्शनं व्याख्याति, यस्त्विति । यस्तु ब्रह्मवित् सर्व्वाणि भूतानि मायापरिणामानि जगद्वस्तूनि आत्मनि आत्मस्वरूपेण यद्ब्रह्म मयि चित्स्वरूपेणा-त्मनावतिष्ठते तदेव मायारूपेण सर्व्वभूतानीति अनुपश्यति उपलभते । सर्व्व-भूतेषु च आत्मानं भूते भूते य आत्मा चिद्रूपः स एव ममात्मा घटपटादि-ष्वाकाशवत् । यथा घटपटादिभेदे प्रत्युत आकाशभेदो न स्यात् तथा भूतभेदे आत्मभेदो न स्यात् । य एतदुपलभते स ततस्तस्माद् दर्शनाद्वैतदर्शनहेतोः न विजुगुप्सते न निन्दते आत्मनः परं प्रेमास्पदत्वात् । सर्व्वभूतेष्वद्वैताल्मोप-

(१) तैत्तिरीयोपनिषत् २।८।१　　(४) कठोपनिषत् २।२।१२

(२) कठोपनिषत् १।२।२०　　(५) बृहदारण्यकोपनिषत् ३।४।१

(३) कठोपनिषत् १।२।१२　　(६) गीता १८।६१　　(७) मुण्डकोपनिषत् ३।१।७

यस्मिन् सर्वाणि भूतानि आत्मैवाभूट्विजानतः ।
तत्र को मोहः कः शोक एकत्वमनुपश्यतः ॥ ७ ॥

लब्धप्रभावादेव जीवानां निन्दाप्रवृत्तिर्जायते सदा सर्व्वत्र सुखानवाप्तिहेतो: ।
"एको वशी सर्वभूतान्तरात्मा एकं रूपं बहुधा यः करोति । तमात्मस्थं येऽनु-
पश्यन्ति धीरास्तेषां सुखं शाश्वतं नेतरेषां"(१), "आनन्दं ब्रह्मणो विद्वान् न
विभेति कुतश्चन"(२) इत्यादिश्रुतिभ्यः । "यथाकाशस्थितो नित्यं वायुः सर्व्वत्र-
गो महान् । तथा सर्व्वाणि भूतानि मत्स्थानीत्युपधारय'(३), "सर्व्वभूतस्थ-
मात्मानं सर्व्वभूतानि चात्मनि । ईक्षते योगयुक्तात्मा सर्व्वत्र समदर्शनः"(४),
'प्रशान्तमनसं ह्येनं योगिनं सुखमुत्तमम् । उपैति शान्तरजसं ब्रह्मभूतमक-
ल्मषम्'(५) इत्यादिस्मृतिवाक्येभ्यश्च ॥६॥

पूर्व्वमन्त्रार्थमनुवदत्यद्वैतदर्शिनः शोकमोहापगमो विस्पष्टयितु', यस्मिन्निति ।
यस्मिन् आत्मनि सर्व्वाणि भूतानि आत्मा एव अद्वैतात्मतत्त्वमेव अभूत् अनुभूतः ।
विजानतः आत्मतत्त्वस्य एकत्वं अद्वैतं अनुपश्यतः अनुभवितुः पुरुषस्य
तत्र तस्मिन् आत्मनि को मोहः कः शोकः इति सम्बन्धः । अनात्मवित्सु
बहुत्वमनुपश्यत्स्वेव रागद्वेषादिजन्यशोकमोहौ सम्भवतः, न त्वात्मवित्सु
द्वैतविवर्जितेषु निर्म्मलचित्तेष्वकामिषु । "नेह नानास्ति किञ्चन, मृत्योः
स मृत्युं' गच्छति य इह नानेव पश्यति"(६) इति काठकश्रुती बहुलदर्शिनां
मूढानामेव शोकमोहाधीनत्वात् पुनः पुनः संसाराबृत्तिरुच्यते । अद्वैतदर्शिनसु
तदभावात् संसारचक्रादिमुच्यन्ते । "यथोदकं शुद्धे शुद्धमासिक्तं ताद्गीव
भवति । एवं मुनेर्विजानत आत्मा भवति गौतम" (७), "आत्मैव संविश-
त्यात्मनात्मानं य एवं वेद य एवं वेद"(८), "स यो ह वै तत् परमं ब्रह्म वेद ब्रह्मैव
भवति"(९) इत्यादिश्रुतिभ्यः । "आत्मानञ्चेद्विजानीयादयमस्मीति पुरुषः ।
किमिच्छन् कस्य कामाय शरीरमनुसंज्वरेत्" (१०), "तं दुर्दर्शं गूढमनुप्रविष्टं

---

(१) कठोपनिषत् २।२।१२
(२) तैत्तिरीयोपनिषत् २।७।१
(३) गीता ६।६
(४) गीता ६।२९
(५) गीता ६।२७

(६) कठोपनिषत् २।१।११
(७) कठोपनिषत् २।१।१५
(८) माण्डूक्योपनिषत् १२
(९) मुण्डकोपनिषत् ३।२।९
(१०) बृहदारण्यकोपनिषत् ४।४।१२

स पर्य्यगाच्छुक्रमकायमव्रणमस्नाविरं शुद्धमपापविद्धम् ।
कविर्मनीषी परिभूः स्वयम्भूर्याथातथ्यतोऽर्थान् व्यदधात्
शाश्वतीभ्यः समाभ्यः ॥ ८ ॥

गुहाहितं गह्वरेष्ठं पुराणम् । अध्यात्मयोगाधिगमेन देवं मत्वा धीरो हर्षशोकौ
जहाति"(१) इत्यादिभ्यश्च ॥७॥

जगत आत्मरूपत्वं तज्ज्ञानस्य च महत्त्वमुक्त्वा तस्यैवात्मनः शरीरजीवेश्वर-
रूपैः सगुणत्वं कूटस्थरूपेण निर्गुणत्वञ्च दर्शयति, सेति । स आत्मा सगुणः सन्
पर्य्यगात् परिवेष्टितवान् समन्तादाच्छादितवान् शरीररूपेण जीवरूपेण च । कं
पर्य्यगात् ? शुक्रं शुभ्रं रजस्तमोमालिन्यरहितं द्युतिमन्तं । अकायमशरीरं ।
अव्रणमज्वरम् । अस्नाविरं स्नावाः शिरा यस्मिन् न विद्यन्ते तमस्नाविरं शिरा-
रहितं शिरोपलक्षितक्रियासाधनरहितं निष्क्रियमित्यर्थः । शुद्धं पवित्रं । अपाप-
विद्धं धर्म्माधर्म्मादिसंस्कारवर्जितम् । "दिव्यो ह्यमूर्त्तः पुरुषः सबाह्याभ्यन्तरो
ह्यजः । अप्राणो ह्यमनाः शुभ्रो ह्यक्षरात् परतः परः"(२) इतिश्रुतेः । एतानि
ब्रह्मणः स्वरूपलक्षणानि निष्कलभावसूचकानि । यदुक्तं माण्डूक्यश्रुतावात्मन-
श्चतुर्थपादनिर्णये, "अदृश्यमव्यवहार्य्यमग्राह्यमलक्षणमचिन्त्यमव्यपदेश्यमेकात्म-
प्रत्ययसारं प्रपञ्चोपशमं शान्तं शिवमद्वैतं चतुर्थं मन्यन्ते"(३) । निर्गुणः स
शुद्धचिद्रूप आत्मा सगुणेनात्मना जाग्रत्स्वप्नसुषुप्तिलक्षणैस्त्रिभिः शरीरैराच्छा-
द्यते । एवमाच्छादितोऽपि स आत्मा अशरीर एव शरीराधिष्ठात्वेऽपि गुण-
सम्बन्धाभावहेतोः शरीरधर्म्मग्रहणासम्भवात् । तदुक्तं छान्दोग्यश्रुतौ, "मघ-
वन्मर्त्तं वा इदं शरीरमात्तं मृत्युना तदस्यामृतस्याशरीरस्यात्मनोऽधिष्ठानम्,
आत्तो वै सशरीरः प्रियाप्रियाभ्याम्, न वै सशरीरस्य सतः प्रियाप्रिययोरप-
हतिरस्त्यशरीरं वाव सन्तं न प्रियाप्रिये स्पृशतः"(४) । आत्मनो निर्गुणकूटस्थ-
रूपेणाशरीरत्वं सगुणजीवरूपेण सशरीरत्वमित्यर्थः । सगुणस्यात्मनः स्वभूत-
गुणक्रियावशाच्छुद्धचिद्रूपत्वं स्वल्पाधिकं प्रच्छन्नीभवति ततश्च जीवत्वं शरीरत्व-
ञ्चोपजायेत । निर्गुणः कूटस्थ आत्मा सगुणस्यैतज्जीवशरीरभावाभ्यामाच्छाद्यते ।
एकमेव तत्त्वं विद्यते नान्यदस्ति किञ्चनेति सर्व्वोपनिषदां मतम् । तच्च ब्रह्म

---

(१) कठोपनिषत् १।२।१२   (३) माण्डूक्योपनिषत् ७

(२) मुण्डकोपनिषत् २।१।२   (४) छान्दोग्योपनिषत् च।१२।१

चिद्रूपम् । ततश्चिद्रूपमिव सर्वं जगत् । सृष्टौ सा चित् प्रतिदेहे पूर्णापूर्णभावाभ्य-
माविर्भवति । पूर्णभावेन सा कूटस्था अपूर्णभावेन जीवः शरीरञ्च । कथं
पूर्णा स भवत्यपूर्णा ? अचिन्त्यशक्तेस्तस्या अनादिसृष्टिशक्तित्वात् । कि
तच्छक्तिश्चिदेव चिद्भिन्ना वा ? चिदेव सा शक्तिः शक्तिशक्तिमत्योरभेदत्वात् ।
कथं चिद्रूपिणी सृष्टिशक्तिरचेतन्यं अखीकरोति ? उक्तमेव ब्रह्मणोऽचिन्त्यशक्ति-
त्वात् । उक्तञ्चैतरेयोपनिषदि, "यदेतद्धृदयं मनश्चैतत् सञ्ज्ञानमाज्ञानं विज्ञानं
प्रज्ञानं मेधा दृष्टिर्धृतिर्मतिर्मनीषा जूतिः स्मृतिः संकल्पः क्रतुरसुः कामो वश इति
सर्वाण्येवैतानि प्रज्ञानस्य नामधेयानि भवन्ति । एष ब्रह्मैष इन्द्र एष प्रजापति-
रेति सर्वे देवा इमानि च पञ्च महाभूतानि पृथिवी वायुराकाश आपो ज्योतींषीत्येता-
नीमानि च क्षुद्रमिश्राणीव । बीजानीतराणि चाण्डजानि च जारुजानि च
खेदजानि चोद्भिज्जानि चाश्वा गावः पुरुषा हस्तिनो यत् किञ्चेदं प्राणिजङ्गमं च
पतति च यच्च स्थावरम् । सर्वं तत् प्रज्ञानेत्रं प्रज्ञाने प्रतिष्ठितं प्रज्ञा-
नेत्रो लोकः प्रज्ञा प्रतिष्ठा प्रज्ञानं ब्रह्म"(१)इति । प्रपञ्चस्य यद्व्यवहारिकजडत्वं
तज्जीवानां भोगेच्छारूपकर्मसंस्काराद्भवति । संस्कारवशाज्जीवा भोगमिच्छन्ति,
पुनस्तदिच्छापूरणाय भोग्यप्रपञ्चस्याविर्भावः स्यात् । जीवानामपूर्णचिद्भावत्वादेव
तेषां भोगेच्छा प्रपञ्चे जडत्वभोग्यत्वदर्शनञ्च । ततः संस्कारा एव जीवानामपूर्ण-
चिद्भावत्वस्य कारणानि । ते त्रिगुणात्मिकाश्चित्गुणपरिणामाः । ब्रह्मणो गुणमयी
सृष्टिशक्तिर्मायैव कर्मरूपेण कर्मजन्यसंस्काररूपेण च स्वकीयपूर्णचिद्भाव-
माच्छाद्य जीवादिभावमवाप्नोति । "छन्दांसि यज्ञाः क्रतवो व्रतानि भूतं भव्यं
यच्च वेदा वदन्ति । यस्मान्मायी सृजते विश्वमेतत् तस्मिंश्चान्यो मायया सन्निरुद्धः ।
मायान्तु प्रकृतिं विद्यान्मायिनन्तु महेश्वरम् । तस्यावयवभूतैस्तु व्याप्तं सर्वमिदं
जगत्"(२) इत्यादिश्रुतिभ्यः । एषा ब्रह्मणः सृष्टिलीला । "सोऽकामयत ।
बहु स्यां प्रजायेयेति । स तपोऽतप्यत । स तपस्तप्त्वा । इदं सर्वमसृजत ।
यदिदं किञ्च । तत् सृष्ट्वा तदेवानुप्राविशत्"(३) इतिश्रुतेः कामतः कर्मसंस्का-
रात् तपसो ज्ञानाच्च सृष्टिरित्युपपद्येत । तस्मात् सृष्टिशक्तेर्मायाया मूलप्रकृतेः
सगुणब्रह्मणो वा द्विविधं रूपमस्ति कामरूपं ज्ञानरूपञ्च । कामरूपेण सा
त्रिगुणात्मिका ज्ञानरूपेण चिन्मयी । त्रिगुणात्मिका सा स्थूलसूक्ष्मकारण-
शरीराणां कारणं, चिन्मयी सा शरीराधिष्ठितानां सर्वसंवेदनानां हेतुः ।
त्रिगुणाश्च न चिद्भिन्नाः । प्रलये ते ब्रह्मस्वरूपेण तिष्ठन्ति । "आनीदवातं

---

(१) ऐतरेयोपनिषत् ५।२-३   (२) श्वेताश्वतरोपनिषत् ४।९-१०   (३) तैत्तिरीयोपनिषत् २।६।१

स्वधया तदेकं तस्माद्धान्यन्न परं किं चनास"(१), "सदेव सोम्येदमग्र आसीदेक-
मेवाद्वितीयम्"(२) इत्यादिश्रुतिभ्यः । प्रलयान्तेऽपि ते ईश्वरात्मना साभ्या-
वस्थायां चिद्रूपिणावतिष्ठन्ते यस्मात् सगुणब्रह्मण ईश्वरस्य सर्वज्ञत्वनियन्तृत्वादि-
धर्म्माः । "ते ध्यानयोगानुगता अपश्यन् देवात्मशक्तिं स्वगुणैर्निगूढाम्"(३)
इतिश्रुतिः । ते योगिनः देवात्मिकां ब्रह्मात्मिकां शक्तिं सृष्टिशक्तिं स्वगुणैः स्वभूत-
सत्त्वरजस्तमोगुणैः निगूढाम् गुप्तस्वरूपां अपश्यन् इत्यर्थः । सा च भगवती
शक्तिः सृष्ट्यर्थमंगतः साम्यावस्थामिकरसत्त्वं परित्यज्य विषमत्रिगुणरूपिणावि-
र्भवति स्वीययाचिन्त्यशक्त्या । ततो जगत् यस्मिन् सा पुनः विषम-
गुणसम्बन्धाज्जीवरूपेण भुनक्त्यविषमगुणसम्बन्धादीश्वररूपेण सर्वमेतच्छास्ति ।
न कदाचिद्गुणाश्चिद्विद्वास्तिष्ठन्ति चैतन्यस्य सर्व्वव्यापकत्वात् । ततस्तेषाच्चि-
द्विलक्षणत्वमप्रतिपन्नम् प्रलयान्ते चिद्रूपिणी ब्रह्मण आविर्भावात् पुनः प्रलये
तस्मिन्नवसानाच्च । "उद्गीतमेतत् परमन्तु ब्रह्म तस्मिन्स्वयं सुप्रतिष्ठा-
ऽत्ऱच्च"(४) इतिश्रुतिः । त्वयं भोग्यं भोक्ता प्रेरयितेति यावच्चरं निर्गुणं
ब्रह्म । सगुणस्याल्मनः शरीरभावेन जीवभावेन चाञ्छादयित्वमुक्त्वा नियन्तृत्व-
मुच्यते । कविः क्रान्तदर्शी सर्व्वद्रष्टा । अनेन कारणशरीराधिष्ठात्वं सूचितम् ।
मनीषी मनस ईशिता नियन्ता । अनेन लिङ्गशरीराधिष्ठात्वं सूचितम् । परिभूः
परि समन्तात् सर्व्वेषामुपरि वा भवतीति परिभूः । अनेन स्थूलशरीराधिष्ठात्वमपि
सूचितम् । स्वयंभूः स्वयमेव भवतीति निष्कारणः । ईश्वररूपेण जगद्रूपेण वा
स स्वयमेव भवत्यचिन्त्यशक्तिमत्त्वात् । स ईश्वरो याथातथ्यतः यथाभवितुमर्च्छति
तथा यथातथा याथातथ्याभावो याथातथ्यं तदनुरूपत्व याथातथ्यतः यथोचितभावे-
नार्थान् कामान् परलोकार्थानुष्ठितकर्म्मसंस्कारान् व्यदधात् विभज्य स्थापितवान्
शाश्वतीभ्यो निलाभ्यः समाभ्यः संवत्सरेभ्यः, संवत्सर इत्युपलक्षणं निलाय
कालाभ्येत्यर्थः । अनेन कालस्य नित्यत्वमुक्तम् । "संवत्सरो वै प्रजापतिः ।
तस्यायने दक्षिणञ्चोत्तरञ्च । तद् ये ह वै तदिष्टापूर्त्तं कृतमित्युपासते ते चान्द्रमसमेव
लोकमभिजयन्ते । त एव पुनरावर्त्तन्ते । तस्मादेते ऋषयः प्रजाकामा दक्षिणं
प्रतिपद्यन्ते । अथोत्तरेण तपसा ब्रह्मचर्य्येण श्रद्धया विद्ययात्मानमन्विष्यादित्य-
मभिजयन्ते" (५) इत्यादिप्रश्नोपनिषद्वाक्येषु संवत्सरमासाहोरात्रस्वरूपे
प्रजापतौ जनानां कर्म्माणि व्यवस्थीयन्ते ॥८॥

---

(१) ऋग्वेदसंहिता १०।१२९।२   (३) श्वेताश्वतरोपनिषत् १।३

(२) छान्दोग्योपनिषत् ६।२।१   (४) श्वेताश्वतरोपनिषत् १।७   (५) प्रश्नोपनिषत् १।९-१०

अन्धं तमः प्रविशन्ति येऽविद्यामुपासते ।
ततो भूय इव ते तमो य उ विद्यायां रताः ॥६॥

किंप्रकाराणि तानि कर्म्माणि कुत्र कुत्र च तानि व्यवस्थीयन्ते इति विशेषण
वच्यति, अन्धं तम इत्यादिमन्त्रेषु । द्विविधं हि पारलौकिकं कर्म्म पुनरावर्त्तन-
विधायकममृतत्वविधायकञ्च । यस्तु ब्रह्मविदेतद्दर्शी "सर्वाणि भूतानि आत्मन्ये-
वानुपश्यति सर्वभूतेषु चात्मानं" "यस्मिन् सर्वाणि भूतानि आत्मैवाभूत्" न तस्य
किञ्चित् करणीयं विद्यते प्रयोजनाभावात् परलोकस्पृहाभावात्, स इहैव मुक्तो
भवति । कर्म्माणि कुर्वन्नपि न तस्य कर्म्मबन्ध इत्युक्तं द्वितीयमन्त्रे । "यदा
सर्वे प्रमुच्यन्ते कामा येऽस्य हृदि स्थिताः । अथ मर्त्योंऽमृतो भवत्यत्र ब्रह्म
समश्नुते" (१), "यदा पश्यः पश्यते रुक्मवर्णं कर्त्तारमीशं पुरुषं ब्रह्मयोनिं ।
तदा विद्वान् पुण्यपापे विधूय निरञ्जनः परमं साम्यमुपैति," (२) "आत्मक्रीड
आत्मरतिः क्रियावान् एष ब्रह्मविदां वरिष्ठ"(३), "पर्याप्तकामस्य कृतात्मनस्तु
इहैव सर्वे प्रविलीयन्ते कामाः"(४), "लीना ब्रह्मणि तत्परा योनिमुक्ताः"(५)
इत्यादिश्रुतिभ्यः । "यस्त्वात्मरतिरेव स्यादात्मतृप्तश्च मानवः । आत्मन्येव च
सन्तुष्टस्तस्य कार्यं न विद्यते । नैव तस्य कृतेनार्थो नाकृतेनेह कश्चन । न चास्य
सर्वभूतेषु कश्चिदर्थव्यपाश्रयः" (६) इत्यादिस्मृतिभ्यश्च । न तु नित्यशुद्धबुद्ध-
मुक्तब्रह्मज्ञानि सर्वेषामधिकारः । ज्ञानिनामेव ब्रह्मनिष्ठाज्ञानिनां कर्म्मनिष्ठा ।
यावन्न चित्तशुद्धिस्तावन्न ज्ञानसिद्धिः । यावन्न वासनाचयस्तावन्नचित्तशुद्धिः ।
यावन्न निष्कामकर्म्माभ्यासस्तावन्न वासनाचयः । अतएव मुक्तिकामिनामविदुषां
सर्वथा निष्कामकर्म्माभ्यास एव कर्त्तव्यः । ये त्वविद्वांसो मूढाः स्वर्गवासजन्य-
सुखाभिलाषिणस्ते स्मार्त्तकर्म्माणि फलाभिसन्धित्सया विधायाविद्यायां
वर्त्तन्ते । न तेषां वासनाचयो न संसारनिवृत्तिः । "अविद्यायां बहुधा वर्त्तमाना
वयं कृतार्था इत्यभिमन्यन्ति बालाः । यत् कर्म्मिणो न प्रवेदयन्ति रागात्
तेनातुराः क्षीणलोकाश्च्यवन्ते" (७), "इष्टापूर्त्तं मन्यमाना वरिष्ठं नान्यच्छ्रेयो
वेदयन्ते प्रमूढाः । नाकस्य पृष्ठे ते सुकृतेऽनुभूत्वेमं लोकं हीनतरं वा विशन्ति"(८)

---

(१) कठोपनिषत् २।३।१४   (५) श्वेताश्वतरोपनिषत् १।७

(२) मुण्डकोपनिषत् ३।१।३   (६) गीता ३।१७-१८

(३) मुण्डकोपनिषत् ३।१।४   (७) मुण्डकोपनिषत् १।२।९

(४) मुण्डकोपनिषत् ३।२।२   (८) मुण्डकोपनिषत् १।२।१०

इत्यादिश्रुतिभिः । "आवृतं ज्ञानमेतेन ज्ञानिनो नित्यवैरिणा । कामरूपेण
कौन्तेय दुष्पूरेणानलेन च"(१), "त्रैविद्या मां सोमपाः पूतपापा यज्ञैरिष्ट्वा स्वर्गतिं
प्रार्थयन्ते । ते पुण्यमासाद्य सुरेन्द्रलोकमश्नन्ति दिव्यान् दिवि देवभोगान् ॥ ते
तं भुक्त्वा स्वर्गलोकं विशालं क्षीणे पुण्ये मर्त्यलोकं विशन्ति । एवं त्रयीधर्म-
मनुप्रपन्ना गतागतं कामकामा लभन्ते" (२) इत्यादिस्मृतिभिश्च । ये पुनरवि-
द्वांसो गुरुशास्त्रोद्घासितचित्ताः स्वर्गसुखं खल्वं मन्यमाना ब्रह्मण आनन्दस्वरूपत्वं
विचिन्त्य संसारदुःखस्यात्यन्तिकोच्छेदमिच्छन्तः सर्व्वकर्म्मसूपासितदेवतानां ब्रह्म-
रूपत्वं विभाव्य वर्णाश्रमोचितकर्म्माणीश्वरार्पणबुद्ध्या समाचरन्ति ते ब्रह्मलोकं प्राप्या-
मृता भवन्ति । अतएव द्विविधा हि मोक्षभाजिनः ज्ञानिनः निष्कामकर्म्मिणश्च ।
ज्ञानिन आत्मस्वरूपमवगत्य जीवन्मुक्तावस्थायां प्रतिष्ठिताः सन्तः सुखदुःखे
समे कृत्वान्तरतय आत्मन्येवावतिष्ठन्ते । ते अस्माल्लोकात् प्रेत्य विदेहा-
त्खिद्रूपे ब्रह्मणि विलीयन्ते । निष्कामकर्म्मिण आत्मनि ब्रह्मस्वरूपमनवगल्या-
पि सर्व्वसुखानां दुःखशेषत्वमनुभूय दृष्टानुश्रविकविषयवितृष्णारूपापरवैराग्यमा-
श्रित्य योगमवलम्ब्य निष्कामेन कर्म्मणा क्रममुक्तेः पन्थानमारोहन्ति । तत्र ते
सत्यलोके चित्तशुद्धिवशात् परवैराग्यं सुखदुःखयोः समदर्शनरूपं ब्रह्माद्वैतविज्ञान-
निष्ठमवाप्य कल्पान्ते मुच्यन्ते । उक्तञ्च भगवता वासुदेवेन—"आरुरुक्षोर्मुने-
र्योगं कर्म्म कारणमुच्यते । योगारूढस्य तस्यैव समः कारणमुच्यते" (३), "शुक्ल-
कृष्णे गती ह्येते जगतः शाश्वते मते । एकया यात्यनावृत्तिमन्ययावर्त्तते पुनः ॥
नैते सृती पार्थ जानन् योगी मुह्यति कश्चन । तस्मात् सर्वेषु कालेषु योगयुक्तो
भवार्जुन ॥ वेदेषु यज्ञेषु तपःसु चैव दानेषु यत् पुण्यफलं प्रदिष्टम् । अभ्येति
तत् सर्वमिदं विदित्वा योगी परं स्थानमुपैति चाद्यम्" (४) इत्यादि । "तपः-
श्रद्धे ये ह्युपवसन्त्यरण्ये शान्ता विद्वांसो भैक्षचर्यां चरन्तः । सूर्यद्वारेण ते
विरजाः प्रयान्ति यत्रामृतं स पुरुषो ह्यव्ययात्मा" (५), "ब्रह्मणा सह ते सर्वे संप्राप्ते
प्रतिसञ्चरे । परस्यान्ते कृतात्मानः प्रविशन्ति परं पदम्" (६) इत्यादिश्रुतिस्मृति-
भिश्च । ते विद्वांस दृष्टापूर्तं वरिष्ठं मन्यमानामपि च्यया नत्वद्वयब्रह्मज्ञानात् ।
ननु कथमेषां निष्कामकर्म्मिणां कर्म्मप्रयोजनं ? कर्म्मफलसन्न्यासिनां कर्म्मसन्न्यास
एव युक्तः न कर्म्म यत् निष्कामेण सम्पाद्यमानेऽपि कर्म्मिणः फलज्ञानात् फलमेव

---

(१) गीता ३।३८				(४) गीता ८।२६-२८

(२) गीता ९।२०-२१				(५) मुण्डकोपनिषत् १।२।११

(३) गीता ६।३		(६) ब्रह्मसूत्रचतुर्थाध्यायस्य तृतीयपादैकादशसूत्रभाष्ये श्रीमच्छङ्कराचार्य्यधृतम् श्रुतिवचनम्

प्रयच्छति ब्रह्मलोकवासलचणम् । अस्ति प्रयोजनमविशुद्धचित्तत्वाद्ब्रह्मोपलभ्य-
भावात् । यावच्चित्तमालिन्यं यावन्न ब्रह्मख्यातिस्तावज्जीवानां नैष्कर्म्यं न
सम्भवति । नापि कर्मेन्द्रियनिग्रहान्नैष्कर्म्यं सिद्धति मनसश्चाञ्चल्यात् परमात्मनि
स्थित्यसम्भवाद् विषयसंसर्गात् । एताद्दृशं मनः कर्म करिष्यत्येव मृषा तस्मात्
कर्मेन्द्रियनिग्रहः । भगवतापि कर्मत्यागनिन्दा क्रियते, "कर्मेन्द्रियाणि संयम्य
य आस्ते मनसा स्मरन् । इन्द्रियार्थान् विमूढात्मा मिथ्याचारः स उच्यते"(१),
"नियतं कुरु कर्म त्वं कर्म ज्यायो ह्यकर्मणः" (२), "मा ते सङ्गोऽस्त्वकर्मणि"(३)
इत्यादिषु । फलतः कर्माधिकारिणां कर्मत्यागी चित्तमालिन्यं भृशं वर्द्धत एव
कर्मेन्द्रियव्यापारमुक्तस्य मनसः स्वच्छन्दविषयचिन्तनात् । ननु ब्रह्मस्वरूप-
विचारे तेषां मनस्तिष्ठतु । तन्न अविशुद्धचित्तेन तद्विचारासम्भवात् । यदा तु
विशुद्धचित्ते ब्रह्मज्योतिः स्फुरति तदैव स ज्ञानी स जीवन्मुक्तो विचारेण जीवति ।
अपरेषां मलिनसत्त्वानां कर्मण्येवाधिकारः । "दूरमेते विपरीते विषूची अविद्या
या च विद्येति ज्ञाता" (४) इति श्रुतेः । अत्र विद्याशब्देन ब्रह्मोपलब्धिरुच्यते न
देवताज्ञानमात्रं देवताज्ञानस्याविद्यया समुच्चयसम्भवात् । तच्च कर्म निष्कामे-
निरहरार्पणबुद्ध्या देवताज्ञानेन सम्पादितं चित्तं विशोधयति । येषां भाग्य-
वशेनैव तच्छुद्धिर्भवति ते ज्ञानभूमिकामारुह्य लोकातीतं ब्रह्मपदं प्रविशन्ति ।
येषान्तु न तद्भवति ते ब्रह्मलोकं प्राप्य तत्र कालेन विधौतचित्तमालिन्याज्ज्ञाने
प्रतिष्ठीयन्ते ।

अन्धं तमः आत्मज्योतीरहितं पिठ्यानां धूमादिमार्गं प्रविशन्ति येऽविद्याम्-
ज्ञानमात्मज्ञानपरिपन्थि सकामं देवताज्ञानवर्जितं केवलं कर्म उपासते आच-
रन्ति । "अथ य इमे ग्राम इष्टापूर्तं दत्तमित्युपासते धूममभिसम्भवन्ति धूमा-
द्रातिं रात्रेरपरपचम्परपचाद् यान् षड्दक्षिणैति मासांस्तान् नैते संवत्सरमभि-
प्राप्नुवन्ति । मासेभ्यः पिठलोकं"(५) इत्यादिश्रुतेः । ततस्तस्मात् तमसो भूय
इव अधिकमेव ते तमः प्रविशन्तीतिशेषः । ये उ ये तु विद्यायां देवताज्ञाने
पञ्चाग्निविद्यायां देवतासु ब्रह्मबुद्ध्या रताः परन्तु कर्मत्यागिनः । पिठ्यानपथि
कर्मत्यागिनां गतिः कर्मिणां गत्यपेक्षा मूढतरा भवतीत्यर्थः ॥८॥

---

(१) गीता ३।६   (४) कठोपनिषत् १।२।४

(२) गीता ३।८   (५) छान्दोग्योपनिषत् ५।१०।३ ४

(३) गीता २।४७

अन्यदेवाहुर्विद्ययाऽन्यदाहुरविद्यया ।
इति शुश्रुम धीराणां ये नस्तद्विचचक्षिरे ॥१०॥
विद्यां चाविद्यां च यस्तद्वेदोभयं सह ।
अविद्यया मृत्युं तीर्त्वा विद्ययाऽमृतमश्नुते ॥११॥
अन्धं तमः प्रविशन्ति येऽसम्भूतिमुपासते ।
ततो भूय इव ते तमो य उ सम्भूत्यां रताः ॥१२॥

पृथक्कृतयोर्विद्याविद्ययोरिदं पृथक्फललं समुच्चितयोरपि तयोः परमन्त्रो-
ल्लिखितं पृथक्फललमाचार्य्यो हृतं । अन्यदेव पृथगीवाहुर्वदन्ति विद्यया अन्य-
दाहुरविद्यया । इति मतं शुश्रुम वयं श्रुतवन्तः धीराणां पण्डितानां आचार्य्याणां
ये आचार्य्या नोऽस्मभ्यं तत् विद्याविद्याविषयं विचचक्षिरे व्याख्यातवन्तः ॥१०॥

विद्याविद्ययोरेकत्वानुष्ठानेन महत्फलमुपजायते । तत्फलजनने तयोः
पृथक्त्वेन किं साफल्यमस्ति ? तदुक्तं विद्येति । विद्यां च देवताज्ञानञ्चा-
विद्यां च कर्म्म च यस्तदुभयं विद्याविद्ये वेदाचरति सह एकत्वेन विद्योद्भासिताम-
विद्यामाचरतीत्यर्थः । देवताज्ञानसहकृतं कर्म्म स्वर्गसुखलाभेच्छाविवर्ज्जितं
सन्निष्कामं भवति । तथा सति स निष्कामकर्म्मी अविद्यया कर्म्मणा मृत्युं
तीर्त्वा मृत्युमित्युपलक्षणं जन्ममृत्युचक्रमतिक्रम्य कर्म्मणा चित्तशुद्धिमवाप्य-
भोगेच्छाराहित्याद्भोगचेतस्थूलशरीरसम्बन्धादिमुक्तः सन्नित्यर्थः । विद्यया
देवताज्ञानेन तज्ज्ञानोत्कर्षेण ब्रह्मज्ञानेन च अमृतमपुनराङ्वृत्तिलक्षणं ब्रह्मलोकं
कल्पान्ते मोचञ्च अश्नुते प्राप्नोति । "तद्य इत्थं विदुः ये चेमेऽरण्ये श्रद्धातप
इत्युपासते तेऽर्च्चिषमभिसम्भवन्त्यर्च्चिषोऽहरह्न आपूर्य्यमाणपक्षमापूर्य्यमाणपक्षाद्
यान् षड् दङ्ङेति मासांस्तान् । मासेभ्यः संवत्सरं संवत्सरादादित्यमादित्या-
च्चन्द्रमसं चन्द्रमसो विद्युतं तत्पुरुषोऽमानवः स एनं ब्रह्म गमयत्येष देवयानः
पन्था"(१) इति श्रुतेः ॥११॥

उक्तमर्थं पुनः कार्य्यकारणोपासनव्यपदेशिनोपदिशति, अन्धं तम इति ।
सगुणब्रह्म जगतः कारणं सम्भूतिर्वा । सम्भवति कार्य्यरूपेणाविर्भवतीति सम्भूतिः ।
यच्च कार्य्यं जगत् तदसम्भूतिरकारणम् । उपासनस्थले कार्य्याभिमानिन्यो

(१) छान्दोग्योपनिषत् ५।१०।१-२

अन्यदेवाहुः सम्भवादन्यदाहुरसम्भवात् ।
इति शुश्रुम धीराणां ये नस्तद्विचचक्षिरे ॥१३॥
सम्भूतिञ्च विनाशञ्चैव यस्तद्वेदोभयं सह ।
विनाशेन मृत्युं तीर्त्वा सम्भूत्यामृतमश्नुते ॥१४॥
हिरण्मयेन पात्रेण सत्यस्यापिहितं मुखम् ।
तत्त्वं पूषन्नपावृणु सत्यधर्माय दृष्टये ॥१५॥

देवता एव बोद्ध्या यथाग्निर्वायुरित्यादयः । अन्धं तमः पितृलोकं प्रविशन्ति
ये असम्भूतिं कार्यदेवता अग्न्यादीनुपासते तत्तद्रूपेण तेषामीश्वरस्वरूपमनवगत्य
फलकामनया । ततो भूय एव तमः प्रविशन्ति ये तु सम्भूत्यां जगत्कारणे
सगुणब्रह्मणीश्वरे रताः । देवताज्ञाने सत्यपि ब्रह्मज्ञानविहीनानां कर्म्माधि-
कारिणां तेषां कर्म्मत्यागादघोरतामसिकलोकप्राप्तिः ॥१२॥

सम्भवात् सम्भूतिं सगुणब्रह्मोपासनादिलर्थः । असम्भवादसम्भूतिं कार्य-
देवतानामग्न्यादीनासुपासनादिलर्थः । अन्यत् पूर्व्ववत् ॥१३॥

सम्भूतिं सगुणब्रह्म । विनाशं विनाशं याति यः स विनाशः कार्यवर्गोऽग्न्या-
दयः कार्यदेवताः तान् । विनाश एव यो विनश्यति धर्म्माधर्म्मिणोरभेदात् ।
अन्यत् पूर्व्ववत् ॥१४॥

विद्याविद्ययोः सम्भूत्यसम्भूत्योर्वा समुच्चयकारिणामभृतत्वमुद्दिश्य केन मार्गेण
तदभृतत्वं भवति मृत्युकालीनप्रार्थनाच्छलेन तत् प्रदर्शयति चतुर्भिमन्त्रै-
र्हिरण्मयेनपात्रेणेत्यादिभिः । हिरण्मयेन हिरण्यं ज्योतीरूपं तन्मयेन ज्योति-
र्म्मयेन पात्रेणाच्छादकेन मण्डलेन सत्यस्य ब्रह्मणः । "तस्य ह वा ब्रह्मणो नाम
सत्यं"(१) इतिश्रुतिः । अपिहितमाच्छादितं मुखं मुखोपलक्षितं स्वरूपं ।
"अथ य एषोऽन्तरादित्ये हिरण्मयः पुरुषो दृश्यते हिरण्यश्मश्रुर्हिरण्यकेश
आप्रनखात् सर्व्वएव सुवर्णः"(२) इति श्रुतिः । ज्योतिर्म्मयेन मण्डलेनादित्य-
पुरुषस्य ब्रह्मणः स्वरूपमाच्छादितम् लोकदृष्टिवच्छिवृत्तमित्यर्थः । "आदित्यो
ब्रह्मेत्यादेशः" (३) इति श्रुतिः । तत् मुखं ब्रह्मस्वरूपं त्वं पूषन् कर्म्मफलविधानेन

---

(३) छान्दोग्योपनिषत् ३।२।४   (८) छान्दोग्योपनिषत् ३।१८।१
(४)   ,,   १।६।६

पूषन्नेकर्षे यम सूर्य प्राजापत्य व्यूह रश्मीन् समूह तेजो
यत् ते रूपं कल्याणतमं तत्ते पश्यामि योऽसावसौ
पुरुष: सोऽहमस्मि ॥१६॥

जीवानां पोषक । यदा जीवा: स्थूलशरीरेभ्य उत्क्रामन्ति तदा तदनन्तरं
देव: पूषा तान् स्वस्वकर्मार्जितान् मार्गान् प्रापयति । "वयमु त्वा पथस्पति रथं न
वाजसातये, धिये पूषन्नयुज्महि"(१),"वि पथो वाजसातये चिनुहि वि मृधो जहि,
साधंतामुग्र नो धिय:"(२)."रथो ऋतस्य नी भव"(३), "विश्वा हि माया अवसि
स्वधावो भद्रा ते पूषन्निह रातिरस्तु"(४) इत्यादिश्रुतिभि: । अपावृणु अनाच्छादितं
कुरु । सत्यधर्माय सत्यं धर्मो यस्य सोऽहं सत्यधर्मा तस्मै सत्यधर्माश्रिताय
मह्यम् । किमर्थं ? दृष्टये सत्यस्वरूपस्यादित्यपुरुषस्य प्रत्यक्षत्वाय । अनेन मन्त्रेण
सत्यधर्माणामादित्यपुरुषप्राप्तिरुक्ता । आदित्याच्चे ब्रह्मलोकं गच्छन्ति । "आदित्यं
गच्छत्येतद्वै खलु लोकद्वारं विदुषां प्रपदनम्"(५) इतिश्रुति: । प्रश्नोपनिषद्-
व्युक्तं, "स तेजसि सूर्ये सम्पन्न: । यथा पादोदरस्त्वचा विनिर्मुंच्यते_एवं ह वै स
पाप्मना विनिर्मुंक्त: स साममिरुन्नीयते ब्रह्मलोकं । स एतस्माज्जीवघनात्
परात्परं पुरिशयं पुरुषमीक्षते" (६) इति ॥१५॥

पूष्णो देवस्य कर्मफलदातृत्वं तथा जगन्नियन्तृत्वादिधर्मवत्त्वमाह पूषन्नि-
त्यादिना । हे पूषन् जगत: पोषक ! हे एकर्षे एक ऋषति गच्छतीत्येकर्षि-
रेकाकिगमनकारी । न कोऽपि द्वितीयोऽस्ति यस्य साहचर्येण स जीवानां
मार्गान् विद्ध्यात् । यदा एकर्षिर्नामाग्नि: । "क्रियावन्त: श्रोत्रिया ब्रह्मनिष्ठा:
स्वयं जुह्वत एकर्षिं श्रद्धयन्त:"(७) इतिश्रुति: । स एवाग्निमार्गदेवरूपेण होतारं
तदर्जितब्रह्मलोकं प्रापयति । हे यम! यमयति जीवानां कर्मफलानोति यम: ।
हे सूर्य! आदित्याख्यसूर्यदेवताया इच्छानुसारेण पूषा जीवान् स्वस्वलोकं
प्रापयति अत: स गौरवात् सूर्य एव । यदा जगत्सविता सूर्य: पूषदेवतारूपेण
जीवान् कर्मानुसारेण स्वस्वस्थानि स्थापयति, अत: स सूर्यएव । "यास्ते पूषन्नावो
अन्त: समुद्रे हिरण्ययीरंतरीक्षे चरंति । ताभिर्यासि दूत्यां सूर्यस्य कामिन"(८)

(१) ऋग्वेदसंहिता ६।५३।१   (५) छान्दोग्योपनिषत् ८।६।५
(२)   "   ६।५३।४   (६) प्रश्नोपनिषत् ५।५
(३)   "   ६।५५।१   (७) मुण्डकोपनिषत् ३।२।१०
(४)   "   ६।५५।१   (८) ऋग्वेदसंहिता ६।५८।२

वायुरनिलममृतमथेदं भस्मान्तं शरीरम् ।
ॐ क्रतो स्मर कृतं स्मर क्रतो स्मर कृतं स्मर ॥१७॥
अग्ने नय सुपथा राये अस्मान् विश्वानि देव वयुनानि विद्वान् ।
युयोध्यस्मज्जुहुराणमेनो भूयिष्ठां ते नम-उक्तिं विधेम ॥१८॥

इति शुक्लयजुर्वेदीयेशावास्योपनिषत् समाप्ता ।

इतिश्रुतिः । हे प्राजापत्य ! प्रजापतेरपत्यं पुमानिति प्राजापत्यः प्रजापति-
नन्दनः । कर्मफलप्रापनेन प्रजापालनात् स प्राजापत्यः । उक्तञ्च संहिता-
श्रुतौ –"विमुचो नपात्"(१), विमुचः स्रष्टुः प्रजापतिः पुत्र इत्यर्थः ।
समुद्र संहर प्रशमय तेज आदित्यदेवस्य ज्वालात्मको भावः । तत्ते तव पूष्णः
रूपं कल्याणतमं परममङ्गलास्पदं तत् ते रूपं पश्यामि, यथा पश्यामि तथा
कुर्वित्यर्थः । "शुक्रं ते अन्यद्यजतं ते अन्यद्विषुरूपे अह्नो द्यौरिवासि"(२)
इतिश्रुतिः । प्रार्थकस्य देवतात्मानां दर्शयति योऽसाविति । योऽसौ असौ
पुरुषः सूर्यमण्डलमध्यवर्त्यादित्यपुरुषः सोऽहमस्मि, अतस्तत्प्राप्तिं प्रार्थयामि ।
"य एष आदित्ये पुरुषो दृश्यते सोऽहमस्मि स एवाहमस्मि"(३) इतिश्रुतिः ॥१६॥

पूष्णि प्रार्थनानन्तरं प्राणस्य देहादुत्क्रमणमासन्नं चिन्तयित्वाजीवनमनुष्ठितं
कर्म स्मरति यदनुसारेण परलोकगतिर्भविष्यति, वायुरिति । अथ मृत्युकाले
वायुर्मम स्थूलदेहस्थप्राणरूपो वायुर्देहादुत्क्रान्तः सन्ननिलममृतं मरणरहितो
वायुर्भवत्वितिशेषः सूक्ष्मशरीरस्थप्राणरूपेणैव चिरं तिष्ठतु यथा पुनः स्थूलदेह-
प्राप्तिं स्यात् । इदं शरीरञ्च प्राणस्योत्क्रमणान्ते अग्नौ दग्धं सत् भस्मान्तं भूयात् ।
ॐब्रह्मप्रतीकः प्रणवः सत्यस्वरूपत्वात् सर्वसंकल्पारम्भे उच्चार्यः । हे क्रतो !
आत्मानं सम्बोधयति हे क्रतुमय संकल्पमय त्वं, संकल्पा एव जीवानां जीवत्वकारणं
तस्मात्ते तन्मयाः । स्मर । किं स्मरेत् ? कृतमनुष्ठितं कर्म स्मर । "अथ खलु
क्रतुमयः पुरुषो यथा क्रतुरस्मिंल्लोके भवति तथेतः प्रेत्य भवति" (४) इतिश्रुतिः ।
क्रतो स्मर कृतं स्मरेति पुनरुक्तिरादरार्थम् ॥१७॥

पुनः प्रार्थयति, अग्ने नयेति । हे अग्ने ! यमहं यावज्जीवमीश्वरज्ञानेन
जुहाव । नय गमय सुपथा शोभनेन पुनरावर्त्तनवर्जितेन देवयानमार्गेण ।

(१) ऋग्वेदसंहिता ६।५५।१ (३) छान्दोग्योपनिषत् ४।११।१
(२) ,, ६।५६।१ (४) ,, ३।१४।१

राये धनाय कर्म्मफलप्राप्तये ।　　अस्मान् मामित्यर्थः ।　　विश्वानि सर्व्वाणि ।
हे देव ! द्योतनात्मक ।　वयुनानि कर्म्माणि मयानुष्ठितं कर्म्मसन्तानमित्यर्थः ।
विद्वान् विजानन् ।　　युयोधि विद्वूरयास्मत् मम सकाशात् जुहुराणं प्रवञ्चक-
म्पृतत्त्ववारकमिनं पापं ।　भूयिष्ठां ते तुभ्यं नम उक्तिं नमस्कारवचनं विधेम ।
हे अग्ने ! अहं त्वां भूयोभूयः प्रणमामि मां देवयानपथा ब्रह्मलोकममृतात्मकं
प्रापयेत्यर्थः ॥१८॥

सिद्धान्तभाष्यम् ।

अत्रादेन मन्त्रेण ब्रह्मणो जगन्मयत्वमुक्तं यद्विभाव्य न कोऽपि भोगेष्वाकाङ्क्षां
कुर्व्वीत ।　य आत्मविदिदं ज्ञात्वा सर्व्वेत्वात्मानमेव पश्यन् कर्म्माणि करोति न
तस्य कर्म्मबन्धः स्यात्, स जीवन्मुक्तो भवति, ज्ञानकर्म्मणोर्विरोधोऽपि तस्मिन् जायत
इति द्वितीयमन्त्रार्थः ।　तृतीयेन मन्त्रेणात्मविदां जीवन्मुक्तानां सम्पूर्णविपरीता
नास्तिका आत्महनो जना निर्दिष्टा ये परलोकगत्यभावादिद्दैव पृथिव्यां मृत्योर-
नन्तरं कीटमशकादिरूपेणातिघोरां गतिं प्राप्नुवन्ति ।　नास्तिकानां गतिं
निर्दिश्याक्नो निर्गुणसगुणभावद्वयं सर्व्वेकर्म्माश्रयत्वञ्च रुद्वेिपेणाञ्च चतुर्थे मन्त्रे ।
पञ्चममन्त्रेण तज्ज्ञावद्वयं स्फुटितं ।　षष्ठसप्तममन्त्राभ्यां जीवन्मुक्तस्यात्मज्ञानिनो-
ऽद्वैतदृष्टिश्चित्तशुद्धिश्चोक्ते ।　अष्टममन्त्रेणात्मनः कूटस्थचित्स्वरूपलक्षणानि
जीवेश्वरशरीरूपैः सगुणतटस्थलक्षणानि चोक्तानि ।　नवमादारभ्यचतुर्दशावधि-
भिर्मन्त्रै रविशङ्कचित्तानामल्पज्ञानिनामास्तिकानां द्विविधा गतिरुक्ता ।　तत्रान्धं
तमः प्रविशन्तीत्यादिभिः नवमद्वादशमन्त्राभ्यां सकामकर्म्मिणां कर्म्मत्यागिनऽनधि-
कारिणां कर्म्मत्यागिनाञ्च पुनरावर्त्तनलक्षणा पितृयानगतिरुक्ता ।　एकादश-
चतुर्दशमन्त्राभ्यां ज्ञानकर्म्मसमुच्चयकारिणां सगुणब्रह्मोपासकानां निष्काम-
कर्म्मिणामपुनरावर्त्तनलक्षणा देवयानगतिरुक्ता ।　पञ्चदशादारभ्याष्टादशावधि-
भिर्मन्त्रै मृत्युकालीनप्रार्थनाच्छलेन देवयानमार्गाधिकारिणो देवताज्ञानमात्म-
स्वरूपोपलब्धिश्च दर्शिते ।

इति श्रीसद्गुरुचरणाश्रयसाधकेन सत्यानन्देन विरचितं वाजसने-
येशावास्योपनिषद्भाष्यं समाप्तम् । ॐ गुरुः ॥

ImTheStory.com

Personalized Classic Books in many genre's

Unique gift for kids, partners, friends, colleagues

Customize:

- Character Names

- Upload your own front/back cover images (optional)

- Inscribe a personal message/dedication on the

  inside page (optional)

Customize many titles Including
- Alice in Wonderland
- Romeo and Juliet
- The Wizard of Oz
- A Christmas Carol
- Dracula
- Dr. Jekyll & Mr. Hyde
- And more...

Lightning Source UK Ltd.
Milton Keynes UK
UKHW020629090519

342383UK00015B/1826/P